Searching for the Perfect Woman

New Imago: Series in Theoretical, Clinical, and Applied Psychoanalysis

Series Editor

Jon Mills, Canadian Psychological Association

New Imago: Series in Theoretical, Clinical, and Applied Psychoanalysis is a scholarly and professional publishing imprint devoted to all aspects of psychoanalytic inquiry and research in theoretical, clinical, philosophical, and applied psychoanalysis. It is inclusive in focus, hence fostering a spirit of plurality, respect, and tolerance across the psychoanalytic domain. The series aspires to promote open and thoughtful dialogue across disciplinary and interdisciplinary fields in mental health, the humanities, and the social and behavioral sciences. It furthermore wishes to advance psychoanalytic thought and extend its applications to serve greater society, diverse cultures, and the public at large. The editorial board is comprised of the most noted and celebrated analysts, scholars, and academics in the English speaking world and is representative of every major school in the history of psychoanalytic thought.

Titles in Series:

Desire, Self, Mind, and the Psychotherapies: Unifying Psychological Science and Psychoanalysis, by R. Coleman Curtis

In Freud's Tracks: Conversations from the Journal of European Analysis, edited by Sergio Benvenuto and Anthony Molino

Searching for the Perfect Woman: The Story of a Complete Psychoanalysis, by Vamık D. Volkan with J. Christopher Fowler

Searching for the Perfect Woman

The Story of a Complete Psychoanalysis

VAMIK D. VOLKAN
WITH
J. CHRISTOPHER FOWLER

JASON ARONSON

Lanham • Boulder • New York • Toronto • Plymouth, UK

Published in the United States of America
by Jason Aronson
An imprint of Rowman & Littlefield Publishers, Inc.

A wholly owned subsidiary of
The Rowman & Littlefield Publishing Group, Inc.
4501 Forbes Boulevard, Suite 200, Lanham, Maryland 20706
www.rowmanlittlefield.com

Estover Road, Plymouth PL6 7PY, United Kingdom

British Library Cataloguing in Publication Information Available

Library of Congress Cataloging-in-Publication Data

Volkan, Vamık D., 1932–
Searching for the perfect woman : the story of a complete psychoanalysis / Vamık D. Volkan ; with J. Christopher Fowler.
p. cm. — (New imago: series in theoretical, clinical, and applied psychoanalysis)
Includes bibliographical references and index.
ISBN 978-0-7657-0616-4 (cloth : alk. paper)
ISBN 978-0-7657-0618-8 (electronic)
1. Relationship addiction—Case studies. 2. Man-woman relationships—Psychological aspects—Case studies. 3. Psychosexual disorders—Case studies. 4. Sex addiction—Case studies. I. Fowler, J. Christopher, 1964– II. Title.

RC552.R44V65 2009
616.85'83—dc22 2009005404

Printed in the United States of America

The paper used in this publication meets the minimum requirements of American National Standard for Information Sciences—Permanence of Paper for Printed Library Materials, ANSI/NISO Z39.48-1992.

Contents

Acknowledgments

Thanks go to Liz Thomson, Kathy Arment, and Nancy Warren-Pitha at the Austen Riggs Center for their diligent assistance in preparing this manuscript. Dianna Downing gave much needed editorial help—we are grateful for her help.

Foreword
Exploring the Intertwining of External Wars with Internal Struggles

Vamık Volkan

In early 2003 Edward Shapiro, the Medical Director/CEO of the Austen Riggs Center, and Gerard Fromm, the Director of the Erikson Institute of Research and Education, invited me to Stockbridge, Massachusetts, as the Senior Erik H. Erikson Scholar in Residence at the Center. Accepting their offer I started to spend four months each year in Stockbridge. One of the best known American psychoanalysts, the late Erik H. Erikson, had worked at the Austen Riggs Center and his portrait, drawn by Norman Rockwell, another former Stockbridge resident, hangs on the wall at the entrance to the Medical Office Building, alongside pictures of other prominent psychoanalysts and psychiatrists, also drawn by Rockwell. In the late 1970s, thanks to the efforts of my friend Joseph Montville, a former U.S. diplomat, my wife and I were included among a small group of psychoanalysts, political scientists, anthropologists and philosophers, and their spouses, to participate in an annual week-long retreat with Erik and Joan Erikson for spontaneous interdisciplinary discussions. For this purpose, we gathered at Big Sur, California, and this program lasted for five years until Erik Erikson's age and health would not permit him to continue meeting with us. When I was invited to come to the Austen Riggs Center for the first time in the fall of 2003, my fond memories of the Eriksons, as well as the group's rich interdisciplinary discussions, were rekindled.

Erik Erikson was a key figure in psychoanalysis. He taught us a great deal about our adjustments to our inner and outer worlds throughout different phases of life, as well as about the interplay between our internal psychological processes and events in the outer world (Erikson, 1950, 1964, 1985). In my own way I have followed the path that was cleared by Erik Erikson as I studied individuals in various locations around the globe where wars or war-like conditions created both individual and large-group regressions (Volkan, 1988, 1997, 2004a, 2006a). As I was getting ready to go to the Austen Riggs Center, I was told that one of my tasks would be to join other scholars in the study of individual and societal responses to trauma and the relationship between such responses. I was not surprised. After September 11, 2001, especially in the U.S.A., the focus on trauma studies had become important and necessary.

Hearing what I was expected to do during my scholarship at Riggs, I thought of one of my analysands, a man I named Hamilton. In the early fall of 1986, when he was fifty-seven years old, he began lying on my psychoanalytic couch four times per week. He finished his analysis four years and ten months later in the mid-summer of 1991. Usually much younger individuals, after noticing some emotional problems within themselves, seek psychoanalytic treatment in the hope that their treatment will allow them to live more comfortably for the rest of their lives. As a psychiatrist, I treated individuals of advanced age—some of them in their eighties or nineties—for depression or other psychiatric syndromes. But Hamilton was the oldest person to enter a formal psychoanalysis. He had already traveled through most phases of a "life cycle," the details of which Erik Erikson had described in his contributions to psychoanalysis. Sometimes I wondered what kind of life he would have had during his younger years if he had entered into psychoanalysis much earlier in his life.

In addition to speaking about his own almost six decades of life, Hamilton also spoke about six generations of an American family from the beginning of the American Civil War in 1861 to the end of the Persian Gulf War in 1991, and illustrated clearly how not only an individual's parents' personal trauma, but also ancestors' historical traumas reverberate in the current generation. Our ancestors' suffering during wars, for example, does not disappear when our ancestors die or when wars end, but continues to influence their offspring. Until recently psychoanalysis has not paid much attention to the link between what transpires in the analyst's office and what happens in the historical arena—there are reasons for this.

In 1932 Albert Einstein wrote a letter to the father of psychoanalysis, Sigmund Freud, asking if the new science of psychoanalysis could offer insights that might deliver mankind from the menace of war. In his response to Einstein, Freud (1932) expressed little hope for an end to war and violence, or the role of psychoanalysis in changing human behavior beyond the individual level. While some analysts, such as Jacob Arlow (1973), found cautious optimism in Freud's writings, Freud's general pessimism was mirrored by many of his followers. This, I think, has played a key role in limiting the contributions psychoanalysis has made to international relations in general and the study of the intertwining of the external and internal wars in individual cases.

Another factor in limiting such psychoanalytic contributions, I believe, was the impact of the Holocaust on psychoanalytic practice (Volkan, 2006b). Let me explain: In his early efforts to develop psychoanalytic theories Freud gave up the idea of the primary role of sexual seduction of children coming from the external world in favor of focusing on the stimuli that comes from the child's own wishes and fantasies in the formation psychopathology. Early psychoanalysts followed this tradition. Thus, less emphasis on actual seduction coming from the external world on the developing child's psyche was generalized to de-emphasizing the role of traumatic external events in general. Furthermore, for a long time, the psychological study of the Holocaust was too painful to be carried out by all but a few analysts (Frankl, 1963). The psychological impact of the Holocaust on those who were affected directly and on the human psyche was generally avoided.

Harold Blum's (1985) description of a Jewish patient who came to him for re-analysis illustrates the extent to which mutual resistances may prevail when both the analyst and the analysand belong to the same large group that has been massively traumatized by an external historical event. Blum's patient's first analyst, who was also Jewish, failed to "hear" their large group's shared trauma at the hands of the Nazis in his analysand's material. As a consequence, mutually sanctioned silence and denial pervaded the entire analytic experience, leaving unanalyzed residues of the Holocaust-related issues in the analysand's symptoms.

We can wonder how many Jewish analysts in the USA and elsewhere after World War II were like the former analyst and how many of them, without being aware of it, influenced the application of psychoanalytic treatment in the USA and elsewhere in a way that tended to ignore Holocaust-related external reality. I suggest that that some of them who were very influential in the field of psychoanalysis exaggerated their bias toward a theoretical position called "classical analysis" that focused only on the analysand's internal wishes and fantasies during the analytic treatment. We now know that in post-World War II Germany as well, there has been both German and German-Jewish analyst-supported (unconscious) resistance to exploring the intertwining of internal and external wars and the influence of the Holocaust-related issues on analysands' psyches (Jokl, 1997; Grubrich-Simitis, 1979; Eckstaedt, 1989; Streeck-Fischer, 1999; Kestenberg & Brenner, 1996; Volkan, Ast & Greer, 2002).

Beginning in the early 1950s, well-known psychoanalysts, both in the USA and elsewhere (A. Freud, 1954; Jacobson, 1954; Stone, 1954; Weigert, 1954) began to explore and write papers on a topic that became known as "the widening scope of psychoanalysis." It took some decades for this widening scope to include efforts for analysts' giving up resistances against recalling and re-experiencing the fearful external world of the Nazi-period. By the 1970s more studies of the influence of the Third Reich on the psyche of the survivors (victims and perpetrators) had begun to surface. (For a review of the literature see: Kestenberg & Brenner, 1996; Kogan, 1998; Volkan, Ast & Greer, 2002).

Psychoanalysts with a "classical" orientation began to realize that the specific nature of any given historical event is important when it symbolically becomes a mirror of our pre-oedipal or Oedipal conflicts and our defenses against them. In 1986 Sander Abend wrote "the impact of daily events, *inner as well as outer* (italics added) plays upon our psychic integration and produces those fluctuations of mood, thought, and behavior which are part of our so-called normal personalities" (p. 565). He added that the analyst is constantly affected by shifting internal and external events. He suggested that the analyst cannot simply remain as a pure and non-changing "analyzing instrument."

World events following the collapse of the Soviet Empire, in the former Yugoslavia, in Africa, and elsewhere in the 1990s, and the post-September 11, 2001 world, have brought about an abundance of trauma studies and psychological studies of wars or war-like conditions. Such studies have influenced psychoanalysts to a great extent (Varvin and Volkan, 2003). Some analysts focused their clinical studies on how previous generations' traumas appear in the analysand's symptoms and even play a role in the analysand's resistance to improving in the treatment (Fromm, 2006; Kogan, 2004; Volkan, Ast & Greer, 2002).

In Hamilton's case, societal events greatly influenced his individual psychology. Hamilton taught me about his internal perceptions concerning white masters, black slaves, race relations, prejudices, and splits in the U.S.A. and illustrated how ordinary people internally perceive political leaders and massive movements like wars. As a child, he had "multiple mothers": his biological mother, his paternal grandmother Dolly, and his black nanny Abigail. Having "multiple mothers" in childhood does not necessarily lead to emotional problems in the individual when he or she becomes an adult. But, if "mothers" hate, degrade or fight with each other, the young child cannot put his or her experiences with them on an emotional continuum. In other words, the child cannot integrate his mother experiences. This, in turn, may create difficulty within the child as he or she seeks a cohesive identity. Hamilton had "white" and "black" mothers in the American South, and he could not reconcile seemingly opposite mothering experiences.

By referring to societal events and their mental reflection, I do not mean to bypass Hamilton's own personal traumas that shaped his personal psychology. Hamilton, although known as a charming, successful, and rich industrialist within his community, also had a "secret" life behind the mask of his public persona. As a child, he was physically abused, a frequent visitor to a place which he nicknamed a "torture chamber." As an adult he was driven to find one nurturing woman after another who would soothe his psychological wounds. I was impressed with Hamilton's "pride and determination" in dealing with his internal demons his own way for almost six decades. However, for all his "pride and determination," he paid a high price. In spite of his smiling face, he was not a happy man, but a man exhausted by a "need" to find a perfect woman and never finding her. Toward the end of the fifth decade of his life, he ran out of self-esteem and became depressed, had murderous thoughts and felt "paranoid," at least temporarily, and came to see me.

In order to contribute to trauma studies, especially the role of transgenerational transmission of trauma in the internal worlds of our patients, at Riggs I began writing Hamilton's case during my Senior Erik H. Erikson Scholarship. Soon I realized that I had another motivation to present the total story of his psychoanalysis. When I, as a newly graduated young physician, came to the United States from the Mediterranean island of Cyprus in the late 1950s, psychoanalysis was considered, in general, to be a highly respected and almost noble profession. I became a psychoanalyst. Since then psychoanalysis has lost its standing among medical professionals and the public. I believe that the U.S. healthcare system's "rules and regulations" and methods for treatment reimbursement have played a role in this negative development—obviously among other factors (Pyles, 2003). Today, psychoanalysis is experiencing a kind of "super democracy." There are many theories and techniques that are put under the umbrella of psychoanalysis. Certainly ideas from some of these new "schools" have helped to enrich the mainstream of psychoanalysis; but, the influence of some other "schools," in my mind, have had a destructive influence on the practice of psychoanalysis and, sadly, in the training of younger colleagues. Some present day practitioners do not even believe in the psychodynamic unconscious or do not even wonder about their patients' dreams. Yet, they call their techniques psychoanalytic.

For a long time I thought that one response to the question, "Does psychoanalysis help?" should be psychoanalysts' presentation of detailed total stories of psychoanalytic treatment processes, where often slow but sometimes drastic changes in the analysand's internal world can be documented. I have done my share of this in the past and presented a number of total psychoanalytic case studies (Volkan, 1984, 1987, 1995). Hamilton's case is another example of this kind of response to the inquiry about whether psychoanalysis works or not.

I spent a little over fourty years as a medical schoolteacher and since I wanted and had time to investigate my own psychoanalytic work and share it with my students, I kept detailed written reports of each session with most of my analysands. This book is based on such extensive data and it is a true story. In writing Hamilton's case, I focused on therapeutic stories instead of reporting his or my every verbal or non-verbal communication. In order to "hide" the identities of people mentioned in this book, I have made some modifications to the real details. In making such modifications, I was careful that they would not disturb the actual therapeutic data.

While many of Hamilton's symptoms and behavior patterns were extreme, I think that all readers will find some aspect of themselves in Hamilton, as I did. Hamilton's story is a universal one, teaching us how our real and fantasized childhood experiences—especially the traumatic ones, specific relationships with parents and others in our early environment, as well as our ancestors' historical events—shape our personalities. We are reminded once more that we cannot choose our parents and the historical time of our births, but we can accept the utmost responsibility as to how we treat our own offspring, making sure that they do not visit a "torture chamber" as the child Hamilton frequently did. The reader, I hope, will be fascinated and moved as I was with Hamilton's courageous struggle to get well.

This book can be read by anyone, who wishes to know what happens when someone visits a psychoanalyst many times a week for years. It can also be used as an "educational tool" for instructors and students of psychoanalysis. When a student is training to be a surgeon, besides reading about the procedure of an operation he or she actually observes a senior surgeon in the operating room and often assists the experienced instructor. Such a "luxury" is not available for a student who is learning to analyze someone on the couch. Traditionally the student receives supervision from a senior colleague for his or her initial cases. But, being in the same room with an experienced psychoanalyst while he or she is performing a "psychoanalytic procedure" or assisting the senior person during the psychoanalytic process is not possible. There is a possibility for a student to watch an analysis conducted behind a one-way mirror. But conducting psychoanalysis while others observe the process complicates the therapeutic action in various ways including interfering with the therapeutic "intimacy" (which technically is called the transference-countertransference axis) necessary for a psychoanalytic work. When I wrote Hamilton's total analysis I thought that going over the manuscript with a student during a series of meetings and responding to his or her questions about my theoretical concepts and technical considerations would be an effective way to teach.

In this book an experienced therapist, clinical researcher and educator, Dr. Christopher Fowler, plays the role of a student. Because of his background and experience he is, I believe, someone who asks more challenging questions. In this book he joins me in providing answers about a years-long process that is called psychoanalysis.

How to Read the Story
J. Christopher Fowler

The story of Hamilton's psychoanalysis with Dr. Volkan can be read to catch a glimpse into the inner world of one man and to gain a sense of how psychoanalysis can help change a life. Like all good stories, reading *Searching for the Perfect Woman* as a piece of prose is a moving experience—disturbing, puzzling, stirring, and ultimately redemptive. As prose, the reader is free to fall into this true story of Hamilton's life and the course of his analysis—to puzzle over how he survived and came to be a troubled man. The reader is invited to join, quarrel with, and question Dr. Volkan's techniques, and to imagine what caused the changes in Hamilton's life. The story is true in that Hamilton's inner life, fantasies, love objects, symptoms, and defenses have not been altered in the slightest. What has been modified, hidden, masked, and distorted are the names and external details of his life. In this way Dr. Volkan provides "protective custody" for Hamilton's social identity, while staying true to the critical details of his inner world. This is a necessary precaution for any therapist writing about his or her patients. It is a practice borne out of the fundamental confidentiality that is a requisite of all therapeutic relationships.

As a study of psychoanalytic technique, it is a rare opportunity to gain access to a total treatment spanning five years. Rarer still is the opportunity to examine a senior analyst's way of coming to gradually know his patient, his methods for gathering important information, of selecting the most crucial bits of Hamilton's life story among the thousands of ideas and impressions, and his rationale for selecting therapeutic actions. For the serious student, as well as the seriously quizzical, I have joined Dr. Volkan in exploring his understanding and application of the principles of psychoanalysis in Hamilton's treatment. I will raise questions for the reader to contemplate, to formulate, then to compare notes with Dr. Volkan. This approach allows the reader to approach the story as a guide to psychoanalytic treatment while providing the lay reader with a better understanding of what goes on in the mind of an analyst during the psychoanalytic process.

Hamilton's treatment is, of course, one approach to psychoanalysis. Schools of psychoanalysis have expanded from a single monolithic standard to a splintered and sometimes fiercely competitive set of theories and approaches. This book will not attempt a comparative analysis of these schools—that is for another time. Instead, the reader is invited to consider alternatives, to formulate ideas, and to consider the merits of this particular approach to psychoanalysis. While differences abound, psychoanalytic treatments are founded on the principles of a dynamic unconscious mental life that supports and thwarts the development of wishes, fears, and the conflicts of living. Most analysts rely on a systematic evaluation of the prospective patient's history, including a complete spectrum of specific external/historical events, internal psychological processes, and their interaction. This total history can sometimes only be known at the termination of a treatment. At the outset, the analyst must be content with gathering a good enough history through the process of a consultation so that psychoanalytic insights can be incorporated into the basic historical facts and current modes of functioning.

Every patient attempts to find ways to deal with his or her internal conflicts and the anxiety such conflicts produce. This is the major reason why patients "resist" the treatment at the same time that they pay money and are willing to spend energy to come to analysis. They, mostly without being aware of it, do not wish to give up their way of handling their internal problems. The patient transfers to the analyst the realistic or fantasized images of important persons from his or her life during the developmental years when the patient's internal structure was being formed through interactions. This is known as transference. During his seminars I noticed that Dr. Volkan uses a Turkish word, "pişmiş" (pronounced pishmish), in describing what Sigmund Freud (Freud, 1912) referred to as the transference neurosis. The word pişmiş, which is now used by many young therapists at the Austen Riggs Center, means "cooked well" or "ripened." Today analysts also analyze patients who are not simply neurotic. Such patients may have problems in their personality organizations and are referred to technically as having "borderline" personality organization or "narcissistic" personality organization. When their transferences become "hot" or "ripe" during the analytic treatment we cannot simply call such situations "transference neurosis." The intensity of their transference relationships with their analysts, before it develops into a typical transference neurosis, exhibits other kinds of transferences. In Hamilton's case we will see various types of "pişmiş" transferences. Through such developments the patient brings the beginnings of various types of influences and accompanying feelings to the analyst's office and struggles to re-experience and "reenact" new versions of them until a new and more adaptive outcome is achieved.

Dr. Volkan will take us through the process of analyzing Hamilton, from the initial consultation, setting a frame for the treatment, to claiming Hamilton as his patient. As the treatment progresses, we have the opportunity to witness the creation of "therapeutic stories" as the fulcrum to internal and external changes in Hamilton's functioning. It is a slow, uneven process with setbacks, useful regressions, and therapeutic challenges. My hope is that my ongoing dialogue with Dr. Volkan will help de-mystify the psychoanalytic process and provide the reader with opportunities to reflect on what makes it possible for Hamilton to change and grow.

Chapter 1
Dr. Schreber's Shadow

Some people are addicted to cigarettes; some people are addicted to heroin; some people are addicted to pornography. Hamilton, a fifty-seven-year-old industrialist, told me when I first met him that he was "addicted" to women. A few months prior to coming to see me, he had placed an advertisement in a national magazine that read: "Professional, active, young grandfather seeks kind, accomplished, non-smoking lady who is interested in theater, tennis, family gatherings, and business conversation. Please reply."

The advertisement also included a post-office box address, which soon was filled to overflowing with hundreds of responses and many photographs. Many years earlier Hamilton created a special address book to keep the telephone numbers of 100 women. He sent bouquets of flowers to many of these women each Christmas. If one woman rejected him, he could call and make a date with another. In his mind, having 100 telephone numbers guaranteed that he would not be alone when he needed female company.

Hamilton's "addiction" to women began in his younger years. He was married to his first wife, Della, when he was attending law school. While Hamilton proclaimed in my office that he was "devoted" to Della, he also had other women friends with whom he was sexually involved. He explained that he "needed" to be involved with multiple women at the same time. He called his secretary his "second wife." After leaving his office and before returning home, he would visit his girlfriends in the neighborhood. Della died from viral meningitis in her early thirties after they had been married for fourteen years. When she died their older son was in his early teens, their daughter was approaching puberty, and their younger son was only six years old. With the help of servants and friends, Hamilton took care of the children after the death of his wife. He told me that he thought that he could not be emotionally involved with them, but he was "a kind father." He never hit his children, he said, because he was determined never to use severe punishment.

Hamilton remained a bachelor for fifteen years after his wife died. During this time his older son got married and gave Hamilton grandchildren. His daughter, who became an architect, married another architect and moved to California. The couple did not have children and Hamilton called theirs a "hippy" life style. His youngest son moved away to attend a university, eventually settling far from his parental home. Only his older son and family continued to live near by. Hamilton lived alone, accumulating and increasing his number of girlfriends. Two years before I met him, he met Mary, a beautiful young woman with dark hair and dark eyes, working in the allied health profession. He married her a few months after meeting her, and within a year their marriage deteriorated. Mary told Hamilton that he was "crazy" and that he should have his head examined.

Together they went to see a marriage counselor who told Hamilton that he was a selfish man because he was constantly trying to control his wife, but Hamilton thought that the counselor took Mary's side in their marital problems.

Throughout the marriage counseling, Hamilton kept a secret from Mary and the psychiatrist. He had kept Della's ashes in an ordinary-looking box. After his second marriage, he put the box in a closet in his first-floor study. At night he would sleep with Mary in the second floor bedroom. When they fought over some issue at night, he would "sleep" with the ashes of his first wife in the study on the first floor. During his second marriage, he "secretly" still had two women to sleep with!

Some months before Hamilton sought my help, he moved out of the home he shared with Mary. He behaved as if she had kicked him out, which was not the case. He was obsessed with an intense wish to be back with his wife, but at the same time, he was obsessed with thoughts of killing her and her presumed lover. He experienced depressive episodes. His "antidote" for such episodes was to meet more and more new women and to go to bed with them. Indeed, he labeled himself "women addicted" when the frequency of his murderous thoughts about Mary increased.

From the very beginning of our work together, Hamilton could describe certain specific behavior patterns that he thought contributed to his being, what he called, women addicted:

- He had to be with a woman every night, otherwise he was afraid of the dark, sudden noises, or being shot. Whenever he was alone at night, Hamilton told me he became extremely anxious.
- He could not date and/or make love to the same woman two nights in a row. He had to date or make love to a different woman on the second night, and then he could go back to the first woman on the third night. If he were with the same woman two nights in a row, he would become quite frightened.
- When he was first with a woman, he considered her to be an angel. However, the next night, the woman turned into the opposite; the angel became a devil.
- If a woman rejected him he could never give her up. He continued to send flowers to old girlfriends who had rejected him seven or eight years before. Even when one threw his flowers back at him and slammed the door in his face, he could not resist bringing her flowers again.
- In contrast, if a woman pursued him and declared her love, then Hamilton could reject her.
- Hamilton secured constant female company by a variety of means. In one case, he provided a woman a rent-free apartment. Hamilton did not think much about this woman, if at all, unless he was desperate. Then he would visit her and have her as his woman for that particular night.
- He only dated women between the ages of thirty and forty.

- He was attracted to women who had black hair, tanned skin, and slender bodies. He would pursue a woman with these characteristics even if he had just met her in a restaurant where she was waiting on his table.
- Hamilton was a smiling gentleman while dining, wining, dancing, going to the theater or playing tennis with his women. However, any sense of their betrayal would induce a wish to "punish" them. At such times, however, except for making some cynical remarks, he would continue to behave outwardly as a gentleman. Sometimes something trivial would make him feel betrayed. For example, if he took a new woman to an expensive restaurant and she did not have proper table manners he would feel betrayed.
- Sometimes, if an ex-girlfriend had a new boyfriend, Hamilton would be haunted by obsessive thoughts of murdering the other man. When having such thoughts, he would also temporarily feel paranoid, as he would when he did not have a woman in his bed. He would, for example, be afraid of walking alone to his car in a dark parking lot.

It was clear that in his mind his girlfriends were interchangeable. To Hamilton, none of his women really had their own identity. They were, for him, "pussy pills" or "titties." He was addicted to such "pills" or nipples; without them he would experience a physiological reaction, feeling dizzy, disorganized, and as if he were paralyzed. His perception of his women as interchangeable manifested in one of his dreams, which he reported to me early in his treatment. In reality Hamilton had attended a costume ball. Many women came to this event wearing colorful garments. That night Hamilton dreamed of being in a big room full of colorful and beautiful birds that were singing for him. Interestingly, he could not distinguish one bird from another.

FOWLER: You describe Hamilton as addicted to women. You also tell us about his peculiar relationship with each woman. What comes to your mind when you hear his stories? How do you distill from the many symptoms and complaints, that which is central to Hamilton's difficulties?

VOLKAN: They say that "curiosity" kills the cat. In the safe environment that I try to provide in my office "curiosity" makes for a good analysis. As I listen to the patient I am curious about the meanings of his symptoms, complaints, and other stories. What comes to my mind has a great deal to do with my training as a psychoanalyst, my knowledge about child development and the evolution of the human mind. For example, when Hamilton speaks about his peculiar need for a woman every night and his being anxious and even "paranoid" without a woman, I wonder if he is stuck in a search of a good mother due to his having difficulties as a small child in his interactions with his mother. When he tells me about not being able to sleep with the same woman two nights in a row or when he describes how during his marriage he went from the bed which he shared with Mary to a couch near Della's ashes I think about his possible inability to integrate his childhood mother's or other important caretaker's mental image. I am curious about these questions, but I do not tell Hamilton this. We just started his analysis. I do not need to tell the patient everything that comes to my mind right away. The patient needs to know that I am listening to him actively. This is why on occasions I make sounds, such as "Hm!, Hm!" In the popular literature cartoonists and comedians make fun of such utterances, but, they are important to let the patient know that I am listening carefully. After all Hamilton will do most of the difficult work during the analytic process. I think of finding ways to help him be curious about the meanings of what he says on the couch as I continue to get information about his life.

FOWLER: When you say that in Hamilton's mind "his girlfriends were interchangeable," is this a dynamic formulation or more simply an observation of his behaviors?

VOLKAN: First, it is an observation I made during the consultation (during the first hour that I saw Hamilton face to face before he started his analysis) and the first sessions on the couch based on his description and stories of so many women in his address book. Then I made an initial or tentative formulation to understand the deeper meaning of his perceiving his many women as interchangeable: What came to my mind was that he was stuck in difficulties in his childhood with his mother or her substitutes. Therefore the women in his adult life (while he obviously knew that they were different persons) stood for "good" and "bad" mothers of his childhood with whom he had unfinished psychological business. He wanted to finish this business; but unfortunately he was stuck repeating the pattern. A short time later, he produced a dream of the costume party with multicolored birds—the dream served as "a proof" that internally he does not distinguish among women! When Hamilton spoke of this dream he was puzzled, "All birds are the same, there are so many but they are all the same." In his daily life, women came and left, so many women that at times he couldn't remember who he had slept with the previous night! It was at this point that I had "a proof" that he was using many women interchangeably. In practice, you always wait to see if the observation from the consultation and from the early hours of psychoanalysis is correct. You wait and listen for data to emerge—perhaps your observations will be accurate and important, perhaps they will be meaningless—the patients will let you know through returning to the themes that are crucial to their conflicts.

After his separation from Mary, he surrounded himself with "birds" or "titties" to soothe his anxiety. But he continually noticed a flame of rage burning inside him. He decided that he needed professional help for his emotional state. He was disappointed with the counselor he saw with Mary because he felt that this man blamed Hamilton for the couple's marital problems and showed no empathy for him.

One day a middle-aged female attorney in his company, who had been very helpful and loyal to him over many years, was visiting his office complex and heard Hamilton speak of his marital difficulties. Normally, Hamilton would avoid discussing his personal issues, but on that day it was obvious to the woman that he was very depressed. She came to his office and after closing the door behind her, told Hamilton that when she was younger she had been analyzed and it had been very helpful. She said that even though it was none of her business, she had noticed his condition and wanted to tell him that he could call her former analyst, who worked nearby, for a consultation. After she left, Hamilton telephoned the attorney's former analyst and told him that he did not wish to see a therapist in the city of Richmond, Virginia, where he lived and worked, because he wanted to seek psychiatric help a distance from his business. This analyst, who knew me professionally, gave Hamilton my name. He told him that I was a "foreigner" and added that if Hamilton did not mind my accent, he was sure Hamilton could work with me since I had a good reputation as a psychoanalyst. His commute to my office in Charlottesville—one hour each way four times a week, combined with his hour in the office with me—would have been a hardship for most people, but as CEO of his own business ventures, it presented no problem for Hamilton. So it happened that Hamilton became my analysand. I had not met Hamilton in person before he came to my office for the first time. I recognized his name when he called for an appointment because shortly before he called me I had read an article about him in a Washington, D.C. newspaper and the style of furniture that was produced in one of his factories.

He arrived looking like a stereotypical English lord, handsome, well dressed, holding himself erect. He had a round face, blond hair, and blue eyes, and except for a slight thickening at his waist, he appeared rather athletic. In fact, he was an avid tennis player. However, his warm smile seemed pasted on his face, as if he had to be pleasant at all times. Soon I learned that not only was he aristocratic in appearance, but in fact he was a distant relative of the Queen of England. His ancestors were related to the British Royalty, although they fought against the British during the American War of Independence. Hamilton was born near Williamsburg, Virginia, where British and United States history are intertwined. Today, Williamsburg is like an open-air museum that is visited by millions of tourists each year, including Americans who come to glimpse their "British" past as well as the birth of their nation. Hamilton belongs to a special group of people who are known as FFV's (First Families of Virginia). While he was very proud of this, his family tradition prohibited him from bragging about it.

His ancestors were also directly involved in the American Civil War (1861-1865), fighting against northern "Yankees." In fact, his ancestors were neighbors of a famous southern political leader. As everyone knows, the South lost the war, and Hamilton's ancestors suffered, losing a great deal of their considerable wealth, prestige and influence in the Virginian society to which they belonged.

FOWLER: Who are you treating? By this I mean to ask, who is Hamilton, psychologically? What vulnerabilities, strengths, and life experiences led him to live this way? Based on the information that you had after the consultation and during the initial weeks of his analysis, how did you develop a working model of Hamilton's problems?

VOLKAN: We all work in systems. There are insurance companies, hospital rules, and legal considerations. We are obliged to come up with a short-hand diagnosis (which is included in DSM IV) when we say we are treating a "borderline patient," or describe Hamilton as having a DSM IV diagnosis. I ask myself the question, "What brings him in now? What is the nature of his internal structure, the nature of his mind and personality organization? I want to know how his internal structure makes him have symptoms, and leads him to make adaptations in his life. It is important that we ask such questions of ourselves (we do not ask the patient to answer such questions—we do not want to burden the patient with such questions because they do not know the answers!), otherwise we would be working without a frame of reference when we start a treatment. As an analyst, I am going to be working with the patient in a very specific intimate way in order to change his internal structures . . . to make him a healthier man. Making a frame of reference is called making a "formulation" about the patient's internal processes. I come up with an initial formulation and then as the analysis progresses I can add to my ideas and modify them as needed. For example, thinking that Hamilton was stuck in searching for a "good" mother is part of a formulation. Of course, at the beginning I know that I'll add much more data to understand his psychodynamics. From the beginning I try to observe patient's repeating behavior patterns in five areas: 1) in the history of the patient's formative years—from childhood through the adolescence passage; 2) in the patient's adult history (past, present, and future); 3) in material that has more direct access into the unconscious (such as through dreams); 4) in the transference; 5) in patient's actions. I also add a sixth area from me: 6) my affective and ideational reactions to the patient.

If I see repeating similar material in all five areas and in my reactions to the patient then I feel like a "scientist." I know that I have "proof" about a patient's way of developing internal structure, personality characteristics, and symptoms responses to a mental conflict which, based on my knowledge on human development, I construct.

Let us go back to my "constructing" the idea that Hamilton had conflicts in the relationship with his mother and developed an inability to have a cohesive image of her. He kept her mental representation as divided in "good" and "bad" categories. This in turn induced in him tensions that, for the rest of his life, he had to deal with these terrible tensions in his own (maladaptive) ways. Very soon you will learn the history of Hamilton's developmental years. You will notice that this history has patterns that are reflected in Hamilton's adult relationships with women, and in the themes expressed in his dreams about birds. Later, after his analysis develops, you will see the same patterns appearing between us (in the transference manifestations) as well as in his actions that include references to our interactions. You will also learn more about my emotional and ideational responses to Hamilton that support my construction of one of his initial conflicts in his dyadic relationships.

Patterns in all six areas may not be available right away. The analyst waits to see them. One more thing, when I say that I become like a "scientist" this statement reflects my love for my profession and my respect for its methodology. I am not speaking about becoming a scientific machine sitting behind the couch. Always there are two human beings during the analytic sessions in the most intimate and emotional relationship.

FOWLER: Then in this form of treatment, the analyst is not primarily concerned about a descriptive psychiatric diagnosis, but the deeper unconscious structures and functions of Hamilton's personality, his fears, traumas, early life history, and the formation of his personality.

VOLKAN: Yes. A patient's initial symptoms or personality traits, even when they appear as bizarre or severe, do not usually predict if this patient's analysis will be difficult or not. It is more important to understand what meanings lie behind these symptoms or personality traits. This is why getting Hamilton to talk about his family and early life history was important. This also helped him to be curious about why he was "addicted" to women, and the meaning of his other symptoms. Some patients don't give a good history initially. That's fine. I'm not going to hit them on the head, barraging them with endless questions. It is much better to get the history from the patient without asking him questions or only asking a few necessary questions (Olinick, 1980). Hamilton had no problems sharing his life history with me.

After I accepted him as an analysand, Hamilton began lying on my couch four times a week. At the time, in early fall, 1986, I was the Medical Director of the University of Virginia's Blue Ridge Hospital in Charlottesville, Virginia. The hospital was located on a beautiful wooded area not far from Thomas Jefferson's home, Monticello. On the grounds of the hospital there were many houses where physicians and their families had lived when Blue Ridge had been a treatment center for individuals suffering from tuberculosis. I had turned one of these small red brick houses into my psychoanalytic office, and here, surrounded by trees and separate from the main hospital building, I saw my analytic patients. Hamilton drove from just north of Richmond where he had his business headquarters, parked his fancy yellow sports car in front of this house and came in to be analyzed. He was much older than most of my other analysands, the owner of diversified holdings, including several factories in and outside of Virginia. He treated me "kindly," lay on my couch and told me whatever came to his mind, as he was instructed. Initially, I felt that I was another employee whom he was paying to listen to him for fifty minutes, four times per week. He was doing his own "analysis." At times I also felt that he was killing me with his "polite" behavior. I charged him my regular fee, in spite of the fact that he was the richest analysand I ever had. In my mind, I did not wish to separate him from my other patients and make him special. I would not learn about his perception about my fee until the fifth year of his analysis.

FOWLER: Why did you decide to charge Hamilton the same fee as your other analysands? What therapeutic benefit is there in attending to the meaning of fees?

VOLKAN: Fees are extremely important (Kubie, 1950). Money serves as a symbol for various internal and external meanings. At one level, fees represent the reality of an analyst's business relationship with his or her patient. Fees provide the reality base behind the transference neurosis or other intense transferences, that the analyst is not the patient's real mother or father. Because I wanted the full meanings of money to be available in the transference, I wanted Hamilton to pay me directly. If a patient brought a check signed by their wives or husbands and so on, I would put the check on the pillow of the couch just before they came to their next sessions. Before lying on the couch they would see the check and say, for example, "What is this? What is going on?" Then I would reply and say something like this: "Our work is only between you and me. This check is signed by a third person. Allow me to keep your analysis between you and me." In Hamilton's case after I received his checks directly, I would forward them to the University of Virginia's Medical Center's business office. Since I was on the faculty of the University's Department of Psychiatry, I was required to do so.

Would there be any circumstance in which I would justify charging him more than my other analysands? No, I would not want to make him special in my mind. During analysis, at one time or another, for the patient money symbolically represents holding back, being generous, and symbolic bodily (mostly anal) functions. My making a special effort to get more money from a patient, I think, would interfere with my understanding what money would mean for the patient. During the analytic process, many analysands play with money as a mental representation of feces. They "forget" to pay you as an expression of their constipation (with its various meanings), for example.

FOWLER: You mentioned that you did not wish to make him special. It was as if you were sensitive to some aspects of his character that needed to be special. Perhaps money could be symbolically representing the gifts he gives to women.

VOLKAN: You are right. You and the reader will be interested to know that Hamilton made himself "special" because I charged my regular fee for his treatment. Later we will see how he made himself special.

During the first year on the couch, Hamilton talked primarily about his relationships with women, sexual matters, and his business affairs. Initially, I listened to him without showing interest in his specific concerns about this or that woman or about his business decisions. My initial impression that Hamilton's women were interchangeable in his mind was repeatedly confirmed—they would be "good" for a while and then "bad" and this pattern would repeat itself with each woman.

In addition, he was obsessed with Mary and a man that he presumed to be her lover. He was not divorced yet and he had to confer with his lawyer often in order to protect himself from Mary and her lawyer. He believed that they were trying to "squeeze out a huge amount of money" from him in the divorce settlement. I gave no advice and I did not try to solve Hamilton's women nor divorce problems.

FOWLER: In many treatment modalities advising the patient becomes part of the therapeutic process. What is the importance of avoiding this in psychoanalysis?

VOLKAN: I am blind to external realities. If a patient tells me that he or she is having trouble with taking a risk with business ventures or with marital problems I do not get involved with the management of such external events. My focus is directed to the intertwining of external events with internal wishes, defenses and adaptations. When analysis helps the patient to learn about this type of intertwining the patient will have a better chance to deal with the disturbing external events more realistically. When I was training to be a psychoanalyst no one taught me how to be an advisor to someone in relation to his or her everyday life problems and no one taught me how to manage somebody's business ventures or marital problems. These are problems for lawyers, financial advisors and other professionals.

Over a year after he started his analysis, his divorce from Mary was finalized, although the divorce settlement was not. A court decision that determined the amount of money he would be required to give Mary took place in the fifth year of his analysis.

Nevertheless, Hamilton also had an "insight" about the genesis of his peculiar relationship with women. This theory included the effect the Civil War had on his ancestors, including his parents, as well as the effects of peculiar child-rearing practices he was exposed to while growing up. His understanding of how his problems were related to things that happened in his childhood was not accompanied by appropriate affects concerning such events.

FOWLER: Hamilton had insights, but no emotional reaction to them. How do you distinguish between an intellectual insight, and insights that show promise for emotional change?

VOLKAN: Hamilton's intellectual knowledge about his past did not lead to his modifying repeated behavior. When there is no emotional insight no true therapeutic change takes place. Hamilton had some "theories" about himself. Some ideas were fundamentally sound, but these theories were isolated from his feelings; therefore, he could only pontificate about them intellectually. If I joined him in this intellectual affair, I would be joining his resistance to change. We could be very smart together, but this would not help him.

FOWLER: In my experience supervising others, joining the intellectualizations is a very common mistake.

VOLKAN: True insight happens when a patient experiences the emotion while telling his or her story especially when it is associated with the "hot" transference. More than that, true insight happens when a patient emotionally struggles to have a different outcome of his or her repeating behavior pattern. Before gaining a true insight about the genesis of his problems, Hamilton created the same story with various characters but with the same outcome. You see, Hamil-

ton was like an author of a play; but under the severe influence of a repetition compulsion—he wrote many plays with many different characters (his women, for example), but his plays were focused on the same story with the same ending. When a patient is free from his repetition compulsion he or she learns flexibility and becomes capable of finishing his or her stories in different ways.

I will now report the story of Hamilton's childhood, his mostly unrepressed memories of his early traumatic experiences, and his emotionless "insight" concerning how such experiences found their way into his adult behavior and feeling patterns.

Hamilton was raised in a family that perpetuated a lifestyle based on the traditions of Southern plantations. As I said, his ancestors had fought for the Confederacy against the northern "Yankees," and when Robert E. Lee's surrender to the North concluded the Civil War, Hamilton's ancestors lost wealth, prestige, and influence. Nevertheless, Hamilton's parents did have a big farmhouse near Williamsburg where Hamilton was born. On the farm, there were other much smaller dwellings for white and black workers and their families. These were the people who oversaw the farm and did its daily work.

When I was a newcomer to the United States in the late 1950s at the University of North Carolina, I received funds from the State of North Carolina. I could pay back my obligation to the state by working for two years in a state mental hospital in North Carolina. As soon as I finished my training in early 1960 I was assigned to Cherry Hospital in Goldsboro, North Carolina. At that time Cherry Hospital was a place that housed only African-American patients with mental problems. As a young man, as the usual saying goes, I had come to America from Cyprus to find "gold." For me "gold' was not to have a financial advancement. I wanted to expand my mind and be exposed to high human ideals in the United States. Instead, my very first job in America put me in an environment where human dignity was lost. I was about to see at close range something called "racism" and the influence of it on people who were subjected to it.

At that time at Cherry Hospital there was not a single African American doctor or a white physician who was born in the United States. The care of the black mental patients was given to immigrant doctors. Many doctors at Cherry Hospital had escaped from communist countries, such as Lithuania or Hungary. I had come to the USA voluntarily. The immigrant and traumatized physicians at Cherry Hospital identified with the African-Americans but also pretended to be "superior" caretakers and perhaps even directed their helpless rage on their patients.

When I was assigned to a place called the "Farm House," a building on a farm away from the main hospital buildings, I had a "laboratory" to observe the symbolic "reenactment" of the aspects of the slavery period of the American history. On the farm, where the "Farm House" stood, chickens were raised, cows were milked, and corn and vegetables were planted. The food at Cherry Hospital was excellent. Patients living in this house worked on the farm. It was thought that they would benefit from this by being involved in a kind of occupational therapy. I had not visited this location until I was assigned to look after the patients in the "Farm House" at the beginning of my second year at the Cherry Hospital. When I entered the "Farm House" I noticed that all the patients, fifty to sixty of them, were black males in their twenties or thirties. They all looked physically healthy. When I first entered the building during visiting hour I noticed many women, mothers, wives or friends, and relatives visiting. There were also many children. The place did not look like a usual mental hospital. It was as if I was witnessing family gatherings at a picnic.

What was most unusual was the presence of an American white man. He was wearing boots and carrying a whip in his hand. Perhaps he was going to tame an animal on the farm. I was told that he was attendant in charge of the farm. When I was introduced to him as the "doctor" for the patients he did not pay much attention to me. I was like a visitor to "his" farm!

I began meeting with each patient individually. I noticed that all of them or at least most of them shared a common "delusion." Each considered himself to be a "Buck." I had no idea what a "Buck" was. Soon I learned that during the slavery period in the United States young and virile black slaves called "Bucks" were assigned to impregnate black slave women in order to increase the slave population. I then understood that the mental patients at the farm shared a defensive adaptation. It was as if they were living during the slavery period of the American history and were working at a farm under a white man with boots and a whip. They were trying to cover up their helplessness and humiliation by "believing" in their being selected for their sexual superiority and breeding purposes. When I saw them with their families and friends indeed they were behaving like "Bucks." (For recent studies of this topic, see: Fogel and Engerman, 1995; Andrews and Fenton, 2001; Follett, 2003; and Gutman, 2003.) Because of my experiences at Cherry Hospital I became interested in learning about the long history of slavery and racism in the United States. When Hamilton talked about his family farm I thought that I had sufficient knowledge about his ancestors' culture.

Hamilton was the third child in his family. He had a brother six years older and a sister four years older than he. But he was the baby for only eighteen months before his mother gave birth to a girl and eighteen months later, another baby sister. By the time he reached age three, Hamilton had dealt with his mother's two pregnancies and the births of two younger siblings. He told me that he felt rejected by his mother.

Abigail, an African-American woman, who he thought was most likely in her late teens at the time, was assigned to look after little Hamilton. Abigail adored the boy and treated him as a "little king" in the servants' quarters where she fed and pampered him. He recalled going for walks in the fields with Abigail and seeing rainbows. She would tell him that one day they would find pots of gold at the end of the rainbows. As long as Abigail was able to unconditionally love and take care of little Hamilton, he could, he said, tolerate "losing" his mother to his younger sisters. But, one week, he saw Abigail on Friday and she was gone the following Monday. According to the story that he learned much later, his parents discovered that Abigail was pregnant, and to them, it was unacceptable to keep a servant who was pregnant out of wedlock, so she was quickly dismissed.

When Abigail disappeared, Hamilton was four years old. No one explained Abigail's disappearance and no one, it seems, understood what losing his beloved black nanny meant to him. She was his primary love companion. When she vanished so did the rainbows and bright colors of his life. Hamilton never saw Abigail again, and he became a person who was "loved and abandoned." He would maintain the psychology of being loved and abandoned for the rest of his life and symbolically repeat this pattern.

For example, after separating from Mary, if he made love to a woman, he would not make love to her the next night, and in this way was abandoned by her. Thus, the "abandonments" would be under his control. All his "insights," and all his actions in relation to his insights, were mainly in the service of controlling emotions concerning the traumatic separations of his childhood. I noticed that he was also involved in a life-long search for Abigail. For example, in his adult life, while walking on the streets or dining in restaurants, he would look for women with dark hair and dark skin. Interestingly, he never made any attempt to find out what had happened to the real Abigail. What he longed for was the black nanny's absolute devotion to him. Of course, the nanny's mental image also included a rejecting woman. In time, I would learn that Mary, too, with her black hair and dark eyes stood for Abigail in Hamilton's mind and he made sure that she first loved him and then abandoned him. In his daily life, adult Hamilton was busy putting Abigail's mental representation under his absolute control so that he could get the "love" he needed and, at the same time, he could prevent the hurt inevitable rejections might inflict on him.

Soon after Abigail was fired from the farm, most likely within a few months, Hamilton's family moved from the area near Williamsburg to another location in Virginia, to a new but smaller farm, leaving behind his familiar surroundings. This new farm originally belonged to Hamilton's paternal grandfather who was a neighbor of a famous southern political leader. This second "loss," I assumed, added to the bewilderment of the child already "abandoned" by Abigail. These were times of economic collapse in the United States. It was the time of the Great Depression, which, in Hamilton's family, reactivated the "memories" of the ancestor's suffering after the American Civil War. Stories of the War were constantly retold in Hamilton's family when he was a little boy. In the new farmhouse there were many photographs of his ancestors and some relics of pre-Civil War Virginia, as well as relics from the Civil War itself.

During the Great Depression, Hamilton's father apparently was very anxious. Many immigrants came to his farm and then left. There was chaos. Concern about money was one of the reasons he sold his farm and moved to a smaller one. During the Great Depression Hamilton's mother was also depressed. At the beginning of his analysis, Hamilton did not use the term "depression" when referring to his mother's condition, but much later, we would reconstruct his mother's postpartum depressions after the births of his younger siblings. Early in his analysis however, Hamilton recalled a childhood memory of looking out the window of the big house on the original farm onto a frozen, cold field and feeling all-alone. He said that this was his first memory of life.

I thought that while the colorful rainbows stood for nurturing breasts, the frozen field represented Hamilton's mother's unavailability and depression and the corresponding depression of the little boy. Hamilton's second memory of his life reflects his "adaptation" to this depression. Hamilton had a nickname for his second memory: "The Vision." It is about his going to his parents' bedroom on the second story of the new farmhouse and seeing his mother bathing. The "Vision" specifically refers to his seeing his mother's breasts, which were known to him as a small child as her "titties" or "nanas." They were most beautiful. At the age of fifty-seven, soon after he began his analysis, Hamilton said that he was still overwhelmed with pleasant sensual feelings while recalling his "Vision," but on the couch he exhibited no emotions.

Hamilton's mother was thirty-two years old when he was born. Accordingly, he saw, or at least in his mind he believed that he saw, his mother's breasts while she was bathing when she was in her thirties. My belief was that he had also seen his mother's breasts when she breast-fed his two younger siblings whom he envied. Hamilton thought that his breast-feeding was terminated early and responsibility for his feeding was passed to others, maybe even to Abigail who was in her teens. But he was not sure if this was what really happened. I thought his "memory" of seeing his mother's breasts might play a role in his seeking, as an adult, women in their thirties and forties. Since the adult Hamilton was drawn toward women with dark hair, dark eyes, and/or dark complexions, and even toward women who wore black stockings, it appeared that he had synthesized his "Vision" with the mental representation of Abigail as his idealized love companion. He had to control his idealized love companions since he also perceived them as would-be abandoners.

FOWLER: Could you expand on the themes evoked in Hamilton's farmhouse and "Vision" stories? They appear to be key to an emerging symbolic story about how he relates to women.

VOLKAN: These stories were not part of his intellectual "theories" about the past. They were symbolic expressions—he was not aware of their meanings. These stories were like dreams. For, example, by talking about the cold snow he told me how cold his mother was. His reference to a "rainbow," I thought, symbolically described how wonderful Abigail was. I did not share my understanding of his symbols right away because I wanted to get the analytic process to move on until he would be ready to truly and emotionally assimilate the meaning of such symbols. At this time of our work if I said "your mother was cold," he might respond, "Yes," and we would go nowhere.

FOWLER: I highlight this because the stories meant a great deal to you but to him they seem to be historical facts.

VOLKAN: As I indicated, these particular stories, or "memories" were like a dream. I was getting something directly from his unconscious collecting more data about my "formulation" of what had bothered him.

Hamilton recalled a photograph hanging on the wall in his parents' bedroom in the farmhouse where they had moved when he was four years old. In this picture, his mother was holding him. During and after his childhood, he thought that the photograph reminded him of the Madonna and the Christ child. This picture was the only one hanging on the wall that included the image of any of the children; his siblings' framed pictures were on a table. Hamilton was the only "prince"! As a child, he believed that the photograph of his mother holding him, which was hanging on the wall instead of sitting on the table, signified his importance and his special place in his mother's opinion. I thought it also stood for a reminder that he was a person who had been "loved and abandoned."

Besides little Hamilton's difficulties regarding "separations" from his early love companions, the presence of his paternal grandmother Dolly in the household complicated and drastically stressed his developmental years. Dolly lived nearby and visited Hamilton's houses, the original and the new farmhouse, very often, but especially every Sunday. Adult Hamilton was aware of the fact that Dolly had specific ideas about child rearing. She saw that Hamilton was subjected to the methodology of a "German doctor" who lived in the previous century. Initially, Hamilton did not recall the name of this German doctor, but during the second year of his analysis he came across a reference in a book about Dr. Daniel Gottlob Moritz Schreber (1808-1861), a physician and an instructor in the medical school in Leipzig during the early and mid-eighteen hundreds. Right away he knew that Dolly's mentor was Dr. Schreber.

Let me diverge from Hamilton's personal history and summarize certain facts about Dr. Schreber, who died the year the American Civil War began. Anyone visiting Germany can witness the influence this man had on gardening. Passing through the German countryside by train, for example, a tourist can see certain properties parceled out into small gardens belonging to or rented by different gardeners. The institution known as Schrebergärten is widespread. But this same man who supported the people's joy in gardening is also known as the creator of the "Schreber movement" for achieving health, which includes recommendations for child-rearing. He was, if you will, the Benjamin Spock of his time, although a very harsh one.

Dr. Schreber's son, Daniel Paul Schreber (1842-1911), became a psychotic, and his autobiography reveals details of his hallucinations and other mental conditions (Schreber, 1903). Sigmund Freud read this psychobiography and wrote his interpretations of Daniel Paul's hallucinations, making Daniel Paul's story the most widely known psychiatric case in history (Freud, 1925). As I was studying to become a psychoanalyst, I read this essay on Daniel Paul Schreber, so I knew of Freud's explanation of Dr. Schreber's role in his son's psychosis.

In the 1980s a scholar, Han Israëls, went through the Schreber family records and concluded that Dr. Schreber, after all, was not a tyrant (Israëls, 1989).

This created a controversy in some circles as to whether or not Freud's observations about Daniel Paul were valid or pure fabrications. Some critics of psychoanalysis stated that Daniel Paul's psychotic episodes (and his brother's suicide) should be explained by genetic or physiological findings on schizophrenic disorders. It is beyond my intention here to focus on this debate about Freud's writings. What is clear is that whether Dr. Schreber was a "nice" father or not, his ideas about child-rearing practices had spread and found acceptance in Dolly's mind.

Dr. Schreber had specialized in orthopedics and advocated an educational method for parents and teachers to use during the early years of a child's life. Some of his books are filled with illustrations of mechanical devices to force a child to sit erect, maintain a correct posture, and so on. He also advocated that extreme pressure and coercion be used against the "softness" of life. He suggested punishments, including punishments for a child's improper pronunciations of words or sniffing through the nose while breathing.

In his book, *Das Buch den Gesundheit* (The Book of Health), Dr. Schreber (1893) recommended that a young child be trained in the "art of renouncing." For example, while a child sits on the lap of a nanny, the latter can eat whatever she wants, but should not give a piece of food to the begging child in order to teach the child the art of renouncing.

According to Hamilton's memories, Abigail did not practice Schreber's method and did not teach him the art of renouncing. In his mind, Abigail behaved in an opposite way, overindulging him and gratifying his oral needs. His memories of the traditional Sunday meals, where grandmother Dolly was ever present, indicate extreme discomfort. It was on Sundays when Hamilton was taught the art of renouncing.

Before Sunday gatherings for meals, the whole family would go to church. Dolly saw that all children behaved well and sat erect on church pews. Dolly would give Hamilton a candy to put into his mouth so that he would not talk while in church. Hamilton, as an adult, would still go to church on most Sundays even though he was not a religious man.

After Sunday church service, the family would return home. By that time, black servants would have prepared the dining room. Children, including Hamilton, would sit around a table that was smaller and lower than the adult table. There was always plenty of food. Dolly would dominate the conversation and make everyone listen to her stories of hungry children. Only much later during his analysis, Hamilton and I would understand that "hungry children" in Dolly's stories represented Dolly as a child in Virginia during post-Civil War times. Dolly's talk of kids in China and Africa would spoil Hamilton's appetite, so that every Sunday he would endure a kind of exercise in the art of renouncing.

After the Sunday family meal, Dolly would also lecture her son and daughter-in-law on proper child-rearing practices as advocated by "the German doctor." When he heard these "lectures," little Hamilton knew that it was time for more, but very severe, "renouncing." His mother would leave the dining room, cut suitable branches from a lilac bush in the garden, and then whip little Hamilton until he "renounced" crying. The lilac bush was in his mother's garden where little Hamilton was forced to help his mother Schrebern (some Germans still use this term for "gardening") while his six-year-older brother and cousins were allowed to play ball. He would feel that he was a "sissy." His mother's whipping him was done to strengthen his character.

As if his mother's ritualistic whipping of Hamilton every Sunday was not enough, Dolly's son, Hamilton's father, was also involved in carrying out what Dolly considered to be Dr. Schreber's advice to make a small boy's character strong. Hamilton's father had created a "torture chamber," which was a big bathroom on the second floor of the new farmhouse, not the smaller one where he had his "Vision."

Little Hamilton slept on the first floor in a bed with his older brother in a Spartan room. Sleeping arrangements were made according to Dolly's specifications. Hamilton's sleeping with his older brother was also in the service of building up his character. He was supposed to learn things from his older sibling who was their father's favorite. Instead of learning from his brother about how to be grown-up, little Hamilton felt that he was not welcomed into a man's world. There was no sexual play between the two brothers, but he recalled comparing the size of his penis with the size of his brother's penis. He thought that his own penis was unusually small and this concern haunted him throughout his life. He was forced to sleep with his brother until he was fourteen years old when his brother left home for college. Until they reached puberty both he and his brother were regular visitors to the "torture chamber," a term Hamilton himself used to describe the big bathroom on the second floor of the new farmhouse.

Once there was a library on the second floor in this farmhouse, which, as I already stated, belonged to Hamilton's paternal grandfather. When Hamilton's parents moved there with their children, they turned this library into a huge bathroom. Hamilton's father beat his sons in this room. The father did not use lilac branches, but used his razor strap for this task.

According to the established routine, first his older brother would enter the "torture chamber" at a given time. The door of the bathroom would be closed while his father beat his older brother as Hamilton was forced to wait outside the door for his turn at punishment. He would, of course, wait with anxiety. When his turn came, his father would put the boy's head between his legs and squeeze it. Then he would remove Hamilton's pants and beat the boy on his buttocks while saying: "This hurts me more than it hurts you!" Hamilton did not recall how many times he was beaten, but certainly such beatings were repeated many times. These were children who were told to have high moral standards and love mankind.

During the passage to adolescence, youngsters unconsciously re-examine their relationships with important people from their childhood as a step toward their own adulthood (Blos, 1979). During Hamilton's adolescent passage, he suffered from a knee injury while playing football. The injury was severe enough for him to be hospitalized. An unmarried aunt slept in Hamilton's hospital room in order to take care of the youngster who, because of his injury, could not get out of the bed or walk until his bones were healed. Adult Hamilton recalled his aunt's scantily covered breasts and their "warmth." But the aunt also did something very frightening to her nephew. One day she took the youngster in a wheelchair to the hospital's morgue and showed him fetuses preserved in jars. The "black eyes" of these fetuses, which I believe might also symbolize the "black eyes" of Abigail, remained in Hamilton's mind for years as a symbol of punishment for incestuous desires. At the same time, he was receiving many injections. Also, doctors decided to take his tonsils out while he was in the hospital. As an adult, when he was attracted to women with "black eyes," this attraction functioned like a double-edged sword. It reflected his incestuous desires on one side and the punishment he could receive for such wishes on the other side. After he physically recovered, he returned home and resumed sleeping with his brother.

FOWLER: This is an interesting repetition of the early childhood love and abandonment by mother and Abigail, now involving the aunt. It seems as though this latest repetition solidified a prohibition against incestuous wishes and set in place a lasting fear of castration from the father. What mental processes are involved in the elaboration of this series of memories?

VOLKAN: We can say that in this memory he was "redoing" his childhood. He comes to the adolescent stage of development with the problem of being loved then abandoned by Abigail and his biological mother. Hamilton tries to remedy this by various ways, such as by keeping a "vision" of his mother's warm breast, but on the other hand the mother is very cold and he has no way of integrating the opposite feelings and images. Hamilton experiences a symbolic castration in the hospital: In this memory he finds a big-breasted aunt/mother and then gets symbolically "castrated" in the hospital when she shows him the dead fetuses in the jars. The fear this evoked may be similar to the feelings evoked by the torture chamber. You see, we may hypothesize that Hamilton interpreted his father's punishments as retribution for Hamilton's incestuous wishes for his mother/Abigail. In this adolescent memory, the latest rendition of an idealized, warm mother comes to him, but the result is that there is not resolution to it—just more fear and guilt. At this point in the analysis, we never hear Hamilton speak of his father coming and sitting by him in the hospital, or the mother nursing him back to health. Hamilton did not go through this adolescence passage in a progressive way—his environment did not allow him to rework the earlier traumas. Instead of modifying internal disturbances from his earlier years, the events surrounding his hospitalization solidified and reinforced the old fears of rejection and castration. In order to "adjust" to life without constant tension and anxiety, Hamilton had to split the good mother from the bad/rejecting one. He had to constantly keep them apart in his mind.

After a year or so the older teenager left home and, for the first time, Hamilton slept alone in his home. Having difficulty adjusting to this situation, he started a ritual. He began nightly visits to his next born sibling, Dorothy, who was sleeping in a room next to his. While his sister slept, he would rub his penis on her legs and ejaculate. Sometimes Dorothy would be awake. She never complained to anyone about his nightly visits, but Hamilton himself was so scared by his ritual that he stopped practicing it after about one year.

Later, he was sent to a military school in Maryland where some of his ancestors had gone. After two years in this school, he knew that he could not tolerate the extreme discipline. He felt humiliated by his belief that he could not compete with other cadets. He left the military school, but thought that by doing so he hurt his father's feelings. Eventually, he attended classes at a university in Washington, D.C. and later enrolled in a law school. He was not a very good student, but was able to receive his law degree. He also married Della while he was a university student. He gave up practicing law a couple of years after earning his law degree and, by using a small amount of family money and a bank loan, he opened his first furniture factory in northern Virginia. In this business venture, he was highly successful and eventually he became a very rich industrialist. Also, he became addicted to women.

I learned very early that I would not help him by defining the nature of his childhood traumatic experiences and interpreting the connections between such experiences and his current behavior and feeling patterns. He was already aware of these connections, at least on an intellectual level. In fact, intellectualization was one of his main defenses in the service of controlling his emotions. I knew that, in the long run, what would help Hamilton was to develop a workable but intense transference relationship with me, and then resolve this transference relationship. In psychoanalysis the term "transference" refers to an analysand's experiencing his or her analyst as a representation of important figures from his or her childhood. In other words, Hamilton needed to "re-live" his childhood wishes and fears, and defenses against expression of such wishes and fears, through the emotional stories he would tell me, or show me through his actions, and then he would resolve them. With Hamilton, I knew I had to stay in a psychoanalytic position and wait for the development of his workable but intense transference relationship with me.

FOWLER: Hamilton's treatment will be less about intellectual insight, and more about intense emotional experiences? Could you elaborate on which intense transferences you are considering? Is it Abigail? Father? Mother? Dolly?

VOLKAN: The answer is all of them. We will see that Hamilton will develop a sense of intense transferences to me. These will appear in the hours, and they will appear in different actions. It is most important that an analyst be patient! As a psychoanalyst, I don't interpret everything I see, I let the psychoanalytic processes develop. Creating an analytic space in which Hamilton is free to experience emotions and fantasies, to cast me in the image of a bad mother and a dangerous father, is critical to an analytic treatment. We will discuss this concept in greater depth later. For now, we can be content to "invite" Hamilton to develop an experience of the various transferences by remaining curious, attentive and receptive.

Chapter 2
A Boy in a Mailbox

At the beginning of our work together, I noted that something about Hamilton made me like him. At first, I did not know what this "something" was. Before long, however, I realized that it was his smile before lying on my couch that appealed to me. In spite of his biological age, a few years older than I was, I saw on Hamilton's face a frightened child's plea for help. He had that powerful "helpless appeal" which is sometimes exhibited by depressed individuals. I realized that he induced rescue fantasies in me: I wanted to rescue him from emotional troubles that had haunted him all his life. I was also confident that, due to my training as a psychoanalyst at a reputable psychoanalytic training institute (Washington, D.C. Psychoanalytic Institute) and my previous experiences with many severely disturbed individuals, I could handle my rescue fantasies in a therapeutic way. When he started his analysis in my office, he reported that he was having depressive and paranoid episodes, but in spite of this admission, he did not look sad, withdrawn or suspicious. His body posture was erect. But, as I already stated, I was able to sense his depression.

Hamilton lay on my couch without hesitation after my two diagnostic interviews with him and after I told him, following his inquiry, that I did not have a "quick fix" for his problems, he began coming to his sessions on time and faithfully. He would maintain this commitment throughout his almost five-year analysis. There were a few occasions when he "forgot" his sessions, but there were psychological reasons for those times, which were analyzed. From the very beginning, Hamilton followed my instructions and began to give, what he considered to be, his "free associations." Initially what came to his mind were opposing perceptions about Mary. She was both an "angel" and a "devil." I did not interfere with his obsessive ruminations about her and allowed the natural evolution of the psychoanalytic process to take its course.

Hamilton seemed unable to link his sessions together, and the stories he was telling me lacked continuity. In one session he would speak of an event and introduce a person to me. The next day or the next week, he would re-tell the same event and re-introduce the same individual as if I had not heard of him or her before. I sensed my own irritation and I wanted to say to him: "Why are you reporting something as if you had not already reported it yesterday? Why are you describing Betsy or Smith in detail as if I never heard of them? Do you think I am stupid?" Of course, I asked none of these questions and remained curious about Hamilton's behavior pattern.

FOWLER: You felt irritated by the repetition of Hamilton's monologue, but you didn't say a word about it. Why did you chose to remain silent?

VOLKAN: An analyst often has feelings about what the patient brings to the sessions or what the patient does in and out the analyst's office. I want to help my patients to get rid of their disturbing symptoms and personality characteristics. The primary objective, the reason I am there in the room with the patient is to take part in sculpting the analysand's internal world. If I have something about my internal world that I become aware of and that will disturb this sculpting, I will not overburden the analysand with it. It is up to me to do something about my internal world. My analysand is not my analyst. Now this has changed in some schools of psychoanalytic theory with more dialogue and open disclosure by the analyst. I doubt such activity is necessary or helpful; I don't teach this to my students. I teach that analysts verbalize their internal reactions (always with the tone of inducing curiosity) only when their reaction is part of a therapeutic story that is being observed and only when it would be helpful to verify for the patient that what he or she is experiencing and learning is real. If I were to tell my patient that I am bored or angry, that would not be therapeutic or psychoanalytic as far as I'm concerned.

I began to notice that the analytic sessions did not have an emotional continuity for Hamilton because his day-to-day sense of self did not have continuity. Furthermore, on one level, I too was not the same person for him during each visit. Thus, he told me about an event and a person again and again since, in his experience, he was talking to a different analyst on different days.

I allowed this pattern to continue for several months, during which time I mentally compared what he was doing during his analytic sessions with me with what he did with his "multiple" mothers in his childhood and with his women as an adult, and realized that these behaviors were identical. Everyone, including him, in a sense was chopped up in pieces. He would hold onto some pieces at one time and other pieces at another time. He was not able to put all the pieces of one person or event together. I believed that he was suffering from a personality disorder that is known as "borderline personality," which technically refers to individuals who do not possess a cohesive sense of self and who split their perceptions, thoughts, and feelings about intimate others into separate camps. When I realized this, I was also amazed at how he had managed to become a successful industrialist. Usually individuals who suffer from such a personality organization cannot manage day-to-day business in an effective manner. I marveled at Hamilton's strengths that allowed him to adapt his life to his personality difficulties. I noted that his life was full of rituals—obsessively so. Through these ritualistic activities, he recalled his childhood environment, put it under his "control," and, by modifying what he was repeating, found "solutions" for his anxiety. In this way he could control and hide his personality disorder from his public life. After performing a ritual, he could control his anxiety at least for the time being. He could be "normal" in most of his business relationships unless such relationships were emotionally and symbolically connected with his childhood desires and fears. Only in an intimate relationship could another person recognize his "private world"—his dividing himself and others into different camps, loving and hating someone as if this someone is one person when he or she is loved and another person when he or she is hated. Apparently, Mary had noticed this and called him "crazy." Now, I was noticing it and calling him "my analysand."

FOWLER: When Dr. Volkan calls Hamilton his analysand, he is respectfully claiming Hamilton as a person with whom he has confidence in successfully treating. While Mary views Hamilton as crazy or Borderline (this term is often used in a derisive tone by mental health professionals disturbed by the patient who internally split the image of the therapist into good and bad parts), Dr. Volkan invites Hamilton to bring his distressing inner life to the analysis. Claiming and accepting the total psychology of the patient into the analysis is crucial to a successful treatment—to reject or deny aspects of Hamilton's inner life would perpetuate the splitting and keep Hamilton divided.

He had come to analysis when some of his ritualistic activities became frantic. He needed to find the "good" Abigail each day in a woman, go to bed with her, and the next day he would lose this woman/Abigail through his own will. He would not sleep with her two nights in a row, but after the third day or so he could once more find his idealized childhood companion image in the same woman. Ritualistically, he was chopping himself, his lovers, and me into pieces while, at the same time, having "control" over such behavior. Amazingly, I could also hear and put together the story of his "insight" reported in the first chapter.

Besides his ritualistic activities and his splitting himself and intimate others, his other primary mental defense against experiencing anxiety, depression, or any other disturbing feeling was his intellectualization of the meaning of his troubles (his "insight") and his illusion of not needing anyone else to help him. For him, "needing" another human meant giving up control over his rituals. Thus when his analysis began, he made me a spectator while he was hiding, in a sense, out in the open on my couch. Soon I learned that he was performing a specific ritual before coming to his sessions four times a week. In fact, the ritual had begun after his separation from Mary and it crystallized after he began seeing me.

Early in the morning a "friend," a white man, would pick him up from the small house in a prestigious area of Richmond where he had moved after leaving a much bigger house he had shared with Mary. Hamilton used this man as a chauffeur to drive him to a run-down diner in downtown Richmond for breakfast. Hamilton would not have breakfast with his date, who might still be in his house when he was picked up to be taken to this run-down place. An African-American woman and African-American man who were not married to one another owned the diner. I learned that they were delighted to have Hamilton as a regular customer. After all, a rich man, who was well known in the community, visiting their poor establishment was a big advertisement for them; it helped with the prestige of the place. Hamilton did not pay more money for his breakfast than the regular fare, but the owners saw that he was entertained. The man would tell him a joke or two and the woman would briefly sing for him. Hamilton intellectually knew that the black woman, in his mind, was a mental representation for Abigail and he perceived the black man as Morris, Abigail's brother. In turn, Hamilton, of course, would be the little boy as he was prior to Abigail's dismissal from the farm.

After breakfast Hamilton's "chauffeur" would drive him back to his house where he would undress, sit in a bathtub filled with warm water, and doze off for a time. This would complete his ritual. He would dress like an English aristocrat, go to his office, be a businessman, and then drive for an hour to my office near Monticello four times a week and be an analysand.

I thought that by his daily visits to the diner, he was revisiting his childhood trauma of losing Abigail. In the repetition, the outcome would be revised. Abigail would still be around and under his control. During this repetition, he experienced no separation from Abigail and her brother, Morris. Since he was aware of what he was doing, there was no need for me to "interpret" the meaning of his ritual. What struck me was the fact that while he certainly had knowledge that the African-American woman in reality was not Abigail and the African-American man was not Morris, the owners of this run-down establishment were not simple symbols standing for Hamilton's childhood love objects. They were what Werner and Kaplan (1963) called "protosymbols." A protosymbol, for the individual who has it, is experienced as what it is supposed to represent. On an emotional level Hamilton could not fully differentiate his original childhood love companion from the owners of the diner, at least during the time when he was performing his ritual.

This ritual was one of the most visible ways he resisted submitting himself to analysis to face his uncomfortable childhood feelings that he had when Abigail, whom he had idealized, abandoned him. In other words, as long as Abigail was still available to him he would be spared splitting her image into "loving" and "rejecting" camps. Thus, he would deal with his personality problem and not need my help to analyze it. Of course, all analysands exhibit resistance to analyses. This has been known since Sigmund Freud's discovering of the so-called "talking cure." All patients sense that psychoanalysis will take away their established way of handling mental conflicts and anxiety and force them to face these conflicts and feel unpleasant emotions connected with them. This is why they resist "hearing" the analyst's interpretations of what is going on in their internal worlds. Instead, like Hamilton, they depend on their own way of subduing unpleasant emotions, even though they continue to ask for help, and pay the analyst's fee. The analyst, therefore, has to pay attention to his or her patients' resistances, especially at the beginning of each treatment, and help analysands give up the resistance when they are ready to do so.

Hamilton would come to his sessions after re-finding Abigail through his morning ritual. He would be fed and entertained by her and her brother before taking a nap (dozing off in the bathtub). Thus, Hamilton would create an illusion that there was no traumatic separation from Abigail and, by extension, no separation from his mother after the birth of his younger siblings. By performing this morning ritual, Hamilton guaranteed that during his sessions with me there would be no need to explore his separation anxiety and all the bad feelings that went with it. He would lie on my couch and constantly smile like a nice satisfied little boy. Actually, he would make me a spectator. He would "wipe out" my identity as a psychoanalyst. I sensed that this would help him express his aggression indirectly. But, since he would act like an obedient little boy and tell me about his life story and his "insight" and perform "free associations," I would not punish him.

Some months after he began working with me, I explained, without accusing him, how his morning activities and "free associations" during his sessions were serving his resistance to analytic work. Even while I was explaining this to him, I knew that he would understand what I said only on an intellectual level. He "heard" me, but gave no emotional response and continued with his morning ritual and his style of "free associations," as well as with his "chopping up" of himself, his women, me, and his sessions. Then I repeated out loud that his visiting Abigail and Morris every morning appeared to be a response to an internal "need," and not to a simple "wish." I explained to him that re-finding Abigail each morning was like finding fresh air to breathe, otherwise he would feel choked as if he were in a burning building. I asked him to remain curious about what I had said and to check his mind to see when his motivation for his morning behavior would become a "wish," instead of remaining a "need." I suggested that when his "need" became a "wish," he might be ready to have a "choice," and modify and/or even give up his daily meetings with the representations of his childhood love objects. This made him feel relaxed and more comfortable with me. I was not pushing him. I was emphatically understanding him and showing him choices.

FOWLER: This is an interesting way to interpret a resistance to the awareness of a need. You emphasize the non-accusatory tone, and the offering of eventual choices to deal with his inner world.

VOLKAN: Resistance is not invoked in reaction to any interaction between analyst and patient. The patient does not resist against the analyst, though some inexperienced therapists may take it personally, as if it were a power struggle. The reason the patient resists the analytic process and resists insight is because of their attempt to avoid anxiety and other disturbing feelings such as shame. An analyst cannot order the patient not to resist. Here I think I helped Hamilton "learn" about his resistance without making him prematurely anxious. If I made him prematurely anxious his resistance might increase. Also the way I approached him, I believe, supported our therapeutic alliance.

There seemed to be a possibility of a therapeutic alliance between us, which would permit us to be jointly curious about his internal world. In general, however, he continued to keep me as a spectator, but nevertheless, he felt freer to tell me more details concerning his life as a child on the farm.

He realized that the chauffeur-driven car was like a baby buggy in which he was taken daily to the kitchen where Abigail and other black farm workers were present. In the kitchen, he was treated as a special being. He thought that most likely there were bodily stimulations: he would be touched and hugged by Abigail and others. He recalled that it was Morris's job to clean his buttocks after he defecated. Morris was a few years older than his sister and stayed on the farm after her dismissal. Adult Hamilton also did not know of Morris's whereabouts. It took Hamilton two and a half years to give up his morning ritual and bring his "feces" to me to be cleaned up, as I will describe later.

Now I will turn my attention to another ritual that Hamilton performed when he began to see me. While his going to the diner occurred outside of my office, the second ritual took place in front of me and lasted for about a year. When I initially invited him to lie on my couch, he first sat on it, took his time to slowly untie his shoelaces, take his shoes off, and then lie down. He performed this ritual at each session. First, I made no remarks about his shoe ritual. Then, a few months into his analysis, one day he took more time than usual taking his shoes off while sitting on the couch smiling at me. I waited until he lay down and got settled before wondering, out loud, if removing his shoes had a meaning. He quickly asked if he was doing something wrong, or if he was disobeying me. I responded that all I wanted was for us to be curious about his behavior.

That night he had a dream about a solid piece of polished wood that looked like a tabletop, but it was standing up on end. Hamilton was trying to climb it without wearing his shoes. This was the second dream he had reported since the beginning of his analysis. The first one, told during the first week of his analysis, concerned an image of a black man hanging dead from a rope. Since he did not volunteer to give association to his first dream, I did not pursue investigating it with him because at the time he was busy chopping up his sessions, and I thought that my focusing on his first dream would lead to his increased intellectualization.

VOLKAN: Dream interpretation is one of the major aspects of psychoanalytic treatment. I believe that a treatment that does not focus on a sophisticated exploration of the patient's dreams should not be labeled psychoanalytic. Dreams have multiple meanings. The analyst considers what is "hot" in the analysand's general communications at the time he or she reports a dream and then attempts to integrate the interpretation of the dream into the ongoing exploration of the "hot" issues, especially the transference issues. The first dream in the analysis has received attention by many psychoanalysts. (See, for example, Saul & Sheppard, 1956; Rapaport, 1959; Alptekin, 2006) Generally, it is perceived as a concise summary of the patient's central conflict and /or his main defense mechanisms for dealing with such a conflict. In a theoretical sense the full analysis of such a dream would mean the full analysis of the patient. Therefore, the general guideline was the analyst's noticing the first dream and his or her being curious about it. But the analyst should not attempt to analyze it right away. If the analyst appears in an undisguised way in the patient's first dream it is thought that this illustrates the patient's difficulty in forming symbols and the patient's inability to evolve a workable transference with the analyst who appears in an undisguised fashion in the patient's dream. In the past there was a tendency not to take a patient with a first dream in which the analyst appears himself or herself into analysis and transfer such patient to another analyst. Since today borderline and narcissistic patients are put on a couch this tendency usually is not put in practice. Hamilton's first dream did not include my direct mental representation. In Chapter 3 we will return to Hamilton's first dream and understand its meaning.

This time, without my prodding, he told me what came to his mind concerning his second dream about the polished wood. In fact, he did not use much repression or displacement about the polished wood symbol of his dream. It stood for the footboard of his parents' bed. On occasions, when little Hamilton was ill, he was allowed to sleep in his parents' bedroom in a crib-like bed. This small bed, shorter than the parents' bed, was placed at the end of the latter. All little Hamilton could see while in this small bed was the solid wooden end of his parents' bed. It looked like a polished tabletop on end. If he had a fever or cough, his mother would bring him orange juice and be nice to him while he temporarily remained in the parents' bedroom—rare memories of a caring mother. I understood that his taking his shoes off before lying on my couch represented his wish that I become a caring mother. But it also referred to a barrier (wooden end of the parents' bed) separating him from her. At this point in his analysis, Hamilton did not refer to the barrier as being against his possible incestuous wishes, and I did not bring up such a possibility myself. His focus, and in turn my focus, was on reuniting or separating from the image of a nurturing mother.

FOWLER: As you said, dreams have multiple meanings. You focus primarily on one aspect at this point. Can you elaborate on the rationale for this?

VOLKAN: I am noticing the transference meaning of the dream. Remember, he had this dream after I became curious about his ritual in the session of taking off his shoes! In response to this inquiry, Hamilton dreams about a good mother and a "bad" mother behind a barrier. In the dream he tells me that his mother's opposite images are not integrated. In this dream we see how his mother takes Hamilton into the parents' bedroom and gives him oranges because he is ill. At this time the mother is a "good" mother. But he has an image of the mother behind a barrier, creating an image of her as unavailable and rejecting. The dream gives us clues why Hamilton splits his images of women and also his images of me.

FOWLER: You noticed the internal trajectory of the dream as bringing together and splitting apart the good and bad images of mother. You also explain to the reader that the image of the bed board serves as a barrier against incestuous wishes for the mother, but you do not interpret this. You followed what was hot for Hamilton? I suspect that many therapists, especially less experienced ones, might interpret the dream as primarily related to the Oedipal wish to covet the mother.

VOLKAN: Before a patient's self-representation and the representations of his internalized objects are integrated, the patient cannot truly work on Oedipal issues. At this phase Hamilton is concerned with tensions caused by early failures in mothering. While I hear Oedipal issues in his material, I do not examine the wish and fear of sexually coveting his mother. At this phase of his analysis, such an analysis would be a wild goose chase because Hamilton is struggling with desires to be nurtured.

I had already sensed a similar "barrier" between us soon after Hamilton started his analysis. Of course, while he was lying on my couch I could physically see him, and especially the smile pasted on his face, but he was keeping a distance from me as if he were hiding beneath a "glass bubble."

VOLKAN: The "glass bubble" is a term that I use to refer to a typical and often conscious fantasy of certain individuals who defensively create an illusion of living alone under a protective umbrella and of needing no one. They deny their dependency needs. (For other meanings of this conscious fantasy see: Modell, 1975; Volkan, 1979; Volkan & Ast, 1994).

He wanted to recapture his "Vision" which he told me about during the first months of his analysis, but was afraid of rejection. Accordingly, the distance between the two of us was under his control.

In the middle of his seventh month of his analysis, I had to attend a meeting on a Wednesday morning. During his preceding session, on a Monday morning, I asked him if he could see me on Wednesday afternoon instead of the morning, his usual appointment time. He politely responded by saying that he would like to say "yes," but on Wednesday afternoons he had appointments to see his other psychotherapist in Richmond. What is interesting is that when I heard that he had another therapist, I was not surprised. He was chopping up his sessions and me in a symbolic fashion. Now, he was telling me that he was splitting me into two pieces in a concrete way. I sensed that his second therapist also represented me. Like he had "multiple mothers" (his biological mother and Abigail) and multiple girlfriends, he of course would have multiple therapists who in fact represented "good" and "bad" sides of one caretaker. To this day I do not know who his second "therapist" was. I was not interested in him or her as a person in his or her own right in the real world. I was interested in Hamilton's internal world and his utilizing "splitting" in his relationship with intimate others. I also instinctively knew that his symbolic splitting of my mental representation was one thing and his concrete splitting of me was another thing.

While I could wait to see what he would do with his breakfast or shoe rituals and his symbolic splitting, I knew that I could not function as an analyst if I were concretely only half a person during his sessions. I told him that what he was doing with me was similar to how he was treating his women, about which we would continue to be curious. But, during his sessions with me, I needed to remain as a "total person" in order to analyze him. Accordingly, I told him that he had two choices: (1) to drop his other therapist and have me as his only analyst, or (2) not to accept the first choice and terminate our work together. Somehow, I knew that he would stay with me. In fact, as I learned later, as soon as he returned to Richmond after our session during which I gave him his choices, he went to see his other therapist and said "good-bye." Thus, we continued to work together. But, he experientially knew that I was now a "total" person, and he could only chop me into pieces symbolically. This was one of the most important turning points of his analysis. In fact, Hamilton's analysis actually began on this day, seven months after his first session, when in reality I became a "total" person for him.

Some years later, I presented Hamilton's case and the above incident at a scientific meeting for psychoanalysts. Some of my colleagues told me that they would never do what I did. They would have continued to be a "half analyst" in a concrete way, and at the same time have tried to analyze the patient's splitting of intimate others. A "half analyst" is not good for anyone; I do not agree with their views. Some colleagues also thought that since Hamilton suffered from severe separation anxiety, I should not have threatened him with abandonment. I do not agree with this view either. Hamilton had his own "solutions" to deal with his separation anxiety and the knowledge that he was separating himself secretively from "half" of me. By giving him a choice, I offered him my availability and commitment to him as a "total object." When he stayed with me, he began experiencing me as what analysts call "a new object," differentiated from his childhood images of intimate others. A patient's experiencing the analyst as a "new object" is necessary for therapeutic progress.

VOLKAN: As long as an analysand experiences the analyst as someone representing the analysand's mental images of important individuals from his or her childhood, the analysand "takes in" nothing new when such images are introjected. During the analytic process the analyst therapeutically differentiates himself or herself from the analysand's archaic self and object (others) images and thus becomes a "new object." The differentiated mental image of the analyst competes with the analysand's archaic images until the analysand himself or herself truly separates the "new object" from others and identifies with it in order to "learn" and assimilate new ego functions. (See: Abse and Ewing, 1960; Leowald, 1960; Giovacchini, 1979; Kernberg, 1976; Volkan, 1976).

After I became a "total" analyst, Hamilton would stop at my office door at the end of most of his sessions and say: "Good session!" or "Good analyst!" This, of course, was another ritual. I allowed this behavior to continue for a while without interrupting until I understood what he was doing. On one level, he was giving me a compliment and making me an idealized companion, but on another level, he was degrading me. "Good session" or "Good analyst" sounded like "Good boy." In the past, white Americans called African American men "boy." Hamilton had returned to chopping me into two people, although now he was doing it symbolically. I was a "white" mother while he was on my couch without his shoes, and then he would make me a "black" person as he left my office. When I brought his new ritual to his attention, he recalled having a black dog when he was in his early teens, and having a habit of addressing this animal as "good boy." He gave up this ritual at the office door, but as I will describe later, he returned to it in the fifth year of his analysis and then we understood that there were other meanings connected with this habit.

Meanwhile, Hamilton told me how, for some time, he had been thinking of bringing his "Vision" concerning his mother's breasts to reality. There should be a "Vision Two." He had found and purchased a breast-shaped hill at a location between Richmond and Charlottesville, one of many beautiful rolling and tree-covered hills in this part of Virginia. He sent his men to remove the trees from the breast-shaped hill and cover the ground with grass. After his men did what they were ordered to do, Hamilton told me that the hill really looked like a breast. Hamilton was very much aware that he was creating a huge and beautiful breast. Furthermore, he wanted to build an artist colony on top of this huge hill, where a "nipple" would be. The artist colony was to be an actualization of his original "Vision" and he called it his "Vision Two." The painters', pottery makers' and other artists' creations would be like bountiful milk coming from his mother's breast. Since he was rich, he fantasized about establishing an artist colony with his own private money and presenting it as a gift to the Commonwealth of Virginia. He was attempting to sublimate his conflict about his dependence on and rejection by his mother by creating something beautiful for everyone to appreciate.

On the couch, he continually made plans for his "Vision Two." Again, since he had little repression, there was no need for me to "interpret" the meaning of his preoccupation. Then, in the tenth month of his analysis, a separation occurred between us. I cancelled a few sessions in order to attend a professional conference. When I returned, he told me that while I was away, he heard of a Turkish woman, who was supposedly beautiful with dark hair, in her thirties, and available (Hamilton of course was aware of my accent and knew that I was a Turkish-American) living in another, rather distant city in another state. He flew to this city to meet this woman without really making firm arrangements for finding her. Once more his reality testing was blurred. In this strange city, he searched for this Turkish woman but could not find her. He returned to Virginia and hired some men to go to the top of his hill (the nipple) and flatten it with bulldozers. When I returned and we resumed our work together, he told me that the place where the artist colony was to be built had been bulldozed; it was lowered twenty feet! His rage against rejection by analyst/Turkish woman/Abigail/mother made him "castrate" the nipple where he would have created his "Vision Two."

He had treated me as a transference figure representing his childhood love companion who rejected him. This was the first time I also came to realize fully the degree of his rage. But this transference manifestation, however drastic it was, would not lead to a workable transference story at this phase of his analysis. Soon he behaved as if nothing had happened between us. Once more, I was only a paid spectator. Today, sixteen years after finishing Hamilton's analysis, I occasionally have to drive by Hamilton's hill on my way to visit some friends. I see it is now home to some business establishments and warehouses on its flat top. I admit to a little twinge of "guilt" and amuse myself by thinking, "You see, if you did not go to that particular conference at that particular time, you might be looking at a beautiful artist colony now, instead of another typical American hillside studded with familiar business signs and neon lights."

When I gave a therapeutic response to his drastic, but externalized, rage and tried to elicit curiosity about the meaning of bulldozing the "nipple" instead of "punishing" him as he expected me to do, Hamilton allowed himself to tell me more embarrassing things about his life. This time his recollections were accompanied by some emotions. When I heard his new stories and still did not condemn him, he trusted me more. I learned that when he married his first wife he suffered from premature ejaculation. This did not surprise me because of his anger toward women while desiring them at the same time. In order to cure his premature ejaculations, he had devised his own solution. An older woman, whom he paid, taught him how to be a lover, and how to maintain his erection. Then he could make love to his first wife in a more comfortable manner without fear of premature ejaculation. Psychologically speaking, he was finding a mother or grandmother who would not reject him sexually. In fact, his solution worked, but he had to continually find symbolic mothers—women who looked like Abigail one way or another—to remain sexually active.

From childhood on, he was involved in some kind of incestuous activities. I already reported his nightly visits to his sister Dorothy's room after his brother had left for college. At one level, he was anxious about being alone and created the "needed" other in his sister. On another level, his sexual activity was an expression of his aggression toward those who abandoned him. He related a dream in which he ejaculated on his sister's legs and tummy, but instead of sperm, what came from his penis were bullets. As an adult, he had sex with some close relatives. After the death of his first wife, his sister-in-law came to his house to look after the children. He seduced her and had sex with her. Soon after this, he seduced his step mother-in-law. At the time, his father-in-law was married to a much younger woman. Telling me about having sex with his sister-in-law and his step mother-in-law was difficult for Hamilton. But, once again, he would quickly change the subject and retreat under a metaphorical glass bubble, rendering me a spectator. In any case, this was not yet the time to explore his sexuality with him. I only told him that his relationships with his sister-in-law and mother-in-law had something to do with his search to find a good woman, and his being angry with them because of his expectation that in the long run they would reject or punish him. He already knew this, of course.

Hamilton's parents lived until they were well into their eighties. In fact, both of them were alive and rather healthy when Hamilton's first wife died. According to Hamilton, his daughter looked like her mother and his daughter-in-law reminded him of his Abigail. To "prevent" himself from bringing his childhood "private life" into his children's lives, he kept them at a distance. During the first year of his analysis, Hamilton rarely spoke of them. He would ritualistically visit his older son's home in Virginia on some occasions, as he had done with his aging parents before they died, but could only enjoy the company of his grandchildren. His "hippy" daughter lived with her husband in California and was estranged from her father. His younger son, attending a university in a distant city, rarely called his father.

During the same period of time, I also learned that, at times, he was treating his business affairs in a manner similar to his affairs with women. Since he was not aware of this, I told him about my observations. In spite of his overall success in business, there was a side of him that made him an impulsive buyer. When he symbolically but unconsciously associated a certain stock or factory that was on sale with Abigail or another "angel," he could not say "no" and would impulsively buy it. If he bought a factory, he would then spend money to beautify or improve its productivity. Fortunately, selling the improved factory to someone else for a higher price (abandoning a "love object") was usually possible, and in the process he had become a millionaire. Nevertheless, deep down he was a "gambler," as he called himself. After buying a new factory, he would fantasize an idealized outcome (more milk and money!). But, sometimes he would also feel "paranoid," as if he had stolen somebody's woman and expected punishment. What Hamilton called paranoia was, in fact, an anxiety-provoking Oedipal triumph. In reality, his open references to triangular Oedipal issues and his actual behavior, such as having intercourse with his sister-in-law and step mother-in-law, was in the service of what Bryce Boyer (1983) refers to as "reaching up" to Oedipal issues in order to find "solutions" for his pre-oedipal, separation-individuation problems.

Since he expected that he might be "whipped" (his own words) by his competitors, he had a host of lawyers working for him, and he would often appear in court. I told him that the court was a place where he could express all the injustices he had faced as a child and find witnesses to confirm that he was unjustly punished by his parents. But, of course, he had to pay money to lawyers in order to achieve this. I told him he was also paying money to me so I could hear and witness what he had faced as a child and how he was "whipped." I told him that whenever he was ready he could experience me as more than a "witness" and allow me to take a trip with him into his private world. If he allowed me, I added, we would travel and explore together at his pace. I added that he could warn me at any time if I went too fast.

Thus, at the end of his first year of analysis, Hamilton was able to tell me what he named his "mailbox story." The second farmhouse where he grew up was about a mile away from a public road. At the point on the public road where their driveway began, there was a huge mailbox. When Hamilton was five or six years old, every school day morning he would walk on the driveway a mile with his older brother to the public road. In those days, there were no school buses, and a horse-driven carriage would come and pick up his older sibling and take them, along with children from neighboring farms, to a country school. Of course, at age five, little Hamilton was not yet old enough for school, but he had developed a ritual walk with his sibling to wait for the carriage.

It is clear that his ritualistic behavior patterns dealing with his inner conflicts and their associated anxiety started at an early age. What made his morning ritual bizarre was his relationship with a motherly schoolteacher who happened to catch the school carriage at the same location as Hamilton's older brother. Not having much repression, Hamilton could visualize this schoolteacher wearing a long skirt that covered her legs. While waiting to be picked up, she would sit on the mailbox and spread her skirt on top of it. In a sense, symbolically speaking, the mailbox covered by her skirt would be placed in her tummy. I thought that the mailbox stood for this woman's womb. Little Hamilton figured out that his body would fit in the empty mailbox. He and his older brother would arrive at the end of their driveway before the teacher got there. Hamilton would enter the mailbox and shut the lid, and make no noise while hiding there. When the teacher arrived, she would not know that little Hamilton was in the mailbox. His siblings would not tell the teacher that there was a live being in the mailbox on which she would habitually sit. Little Hamilton, in the darkness, as he recalled on my couch, would have a sensation of being in this woman's belly, at least for some minutes. After everyone left, he would get out of the mailbox and return home. But, the experience as he created it, of being a woman's (mother's/Abigail's) only child would help him to "tolerate" his previous rejections by his love objects. Of course, I do not know in reality how many times little Hamilton hid in the mailbox.

Our examination of the meaning of this story provided me with a storyline for one of Hamilton's most important unconscious fantasies.

FOWLER: Can you say more about the importance of such an unconscious "story"?

VOLKAN: Hamilton's being in a "glass bubble" reflects his unconscious fantasy of being the only child in his mother's belly. The story of the mailbox represents just such a fantasy, in a condensed and somewhat distorted way. Sigmund Freud (1908) noted two types of unconscious fantasies: those that have been unconscious all along and those fantasies that began as conscious daydreams and then were later repressed. Here I am referring to a child's perception and "interpretation" of a childhood trauma that initiates an unconscious fantasy of the second type. Beres (1962) asserted that analysts detect the presence of unconscious fantasies in clinical work when patients report free associations, dreams, and stories involving transference themes. When such fantasies emerge in present mental conflicts they often create intense anxiety. We regularly see individuals who have developed character traits, inhibitions, or symptoms to keep their fantasies unconscious— that is, to keep them repressed (Arlow, 1969; Inderbitzin and Levy, 1990; Volkan and Ast, 1997). For instance, a young man —who, as a child, had developed an unconscious fantasy of killing his unborn sibling—exhibited as an adult the character traits of an explorer; he became a man of the outdoors who obsessively sought out caves to survey. Whenever he came across one, though, he experienced an inhibition or a symptom that prevented him from entering it: either he would feel suddenly reticent about entering the cave before him, or he would experience severe leg cramps. As the caves represented his pregnant mother's abdomen, his inhibition, and symptom enabled him to keep his fantasy repressed—to "not know" his wish to kill the sibling whom he might find within each symbolic womb. On the other hand, an unconscious fantasy's influence on an individual may change; instead of creating anxiety and symptoms, it may become the source of adaptive, altruistic efforts. For example, another individual with an aggressive unconscious fantasy about a sibling may become a good teacher of small children. Returning to Hamilton, we see the unconscious fantasy in the story of the mailbox, and we see it in the way he relates to me when he is most anxious—he does not experience me as an ally at such moments; he must keep me at a great distance while my office, and the couch is the symbol of the womb.

The "unconscious fantasy" I refer to here reflects a child's "summary" of his or her understanding of traumatic experiences by utilizing whatever mental ability he or she has at the time and contaminating this understanding with primary process thinking. The child's desires, fears, feelings, and symbolizing functions are stimulated by the events, and he or she combines them in an illogical "unconscious fantasy." During an analytic process the analyst begins to put a storyline to the previously unconscious summary of the event and make it conscious. When the time comes, the analyst shares the storyline with his or her analysand. Throughout the analytic process the analyst and the analysand reexamine the storyline of the previously unconscious fantasy and make modifications and additions to it when necessary. The analysis of the influence of an unconscious fantasy is required in a proper psychoanalytic treatment process.

My storyline of Hamilton's unconscious fantasy was this: In order not to have his younger siblings and avoid losing his mother's love, he wanted to enter into his mother's tummy and be the only child there. This, of course, would mean that he would "kill" his younger siblings. As I had noticed, this "killing" would be expressed in different ways. For example, he tried to "kill" his next born sister with his semen/bullets, or he tried to "kill" all his siblings by focusing on his recollection that he was the only child who was his mother's darling. His picture with his mother, which looked like the Madonna holding the Christ child, hung on the wall in the parental bedroom while pictures of all his siblings were only put on a table; thus, all siblings were rendered to a secondary position, "killed," in a sense, while he remained "alive" on the wall.

Examining Hamilton's "mailbox" story allowed me to see another meaning in his transference relationship to me during the first year of his analysis. I already mentioned how I felt he was under a "glass bubble" and how he made me a spectator, an outsider. His "mailbox story" would tell us that he had reactivated his unconscious fantasy during his sessions. I told Hamilton that he was "hiding" in his mother's belly (my couch) while making me an outsider who could not intrude into his place where he was alone, but omnipotently special. In my office, he was the only child of the mother, and I was the competitor (siblings, father) who was kept outside, but who might still punish him and remove him from his special unity with his mother.

A psychoanalyst is not a detective in search of actual truth. I search for "psychic truth." Hamilton's recollection of the "mailbox" story reflected his unconscious fantasy, his "psychic truth" that organized his internal psychological world. During the first year of his analysis, he had made my office his childhood mailbox. That was his main transference story and it took a year for us to discover it fully and talk about it. After this, he could allow me to join him in exploring his internal world.

Chapter 3
Inky Messes

After Hamilton recalled his childhood ritual of hiding in a mailbox and after he understood how he had also been "hiding" on my couch, his ways of relating to me underwent drastic changes. I observed his attempts to develop a genuine therapeutic alliance with me and join me in becoming curious about his internal world.

FOWLER: You make reference to the therapeutic alliance several times. I found this particularly interesting because you're outlining something that is different than the popular concept of the positive regard for the therapist, what many refer to as the therapeutic bond. You are articulating the common goal that Hamilton has begun to join, after a year of "hiding," the major transference story.

VOLKAN: If a therapist thinks that he or she has to finish the session with the patient smiling and feeling good about the session, then the therapy is not focusing on the most important thing—the journey into exploring the patient's psyche with them. Many therapists get lost in the desire to be a good, kind, and sweet therapist in order to be a model of "good mothering." Such therapists are prone to avoid the patient's resistances and the patient's aggressive feelings. Such feelings and their causes are subjects for analysis. From the beginning the analyst pays attention to the creation of a therapeutic alliance: Being curious together about what develops between the patient and the analyst rain and shine. One cannot order a patient to have a therapeutic alliance. Its full development is a process. Sometimes the development of a solid therapeutic alliance takes a long time.

FOWLER: I see what you mean—Hamilton was polite and conscientious, attended sessions, and did not get into power struggles; yet, he was not yet using you because he was protecting himself in a glass bubble. This is the first mention of Hamilton joining you in the curiosity about himself. So you are defining therapeutic alliance as an active interest in his psychic reality.

VOLKAN: Yes, we are going to take a trip together. During this mutual work I try to focus on his current states and fantasies. If we extend the metaphor of a journey, I will not walk in front of Hamilton, and I will not walk behind him. Since I know that this journey is the most important thing in Hamilton's life, he comes to recognize this too.

Nevertheless, at the beginning of his second year of analysis, he needed to repeat once more, in action, his childhood wishes, fears, and fantasies concerning the birth of his younger siblings, his finding an idealized mother, and her inevitable rejection. First, he kept this repetition a secret from me. But, after his frantic activities were over and he settled down in a thoughtful way and with appropriate emotion, he shared his observations about what he had done. I sensed that he was beginning to master his conflict about his separations from mother/Abigail.

His activities, which were initially kept hidden from me, began when he invited the members of his family and some friends to a special birthday celebration. It happens that the birthdays of his daughter and daughter-in-law fall within a short span of time. Hamilton made a decision that this year two birthdays should be celebrated together one Sunday afternoon. His daughter and her husband would fly from California to Virginia for this occasion. He would take care of all the expenses. What he kept as a "secret" from me—and to a great extent from himself—was the fact that his "two birthdays into one" was an attempt to bravely face his trauma over his younger siblings' births.

As the date of the birthday gathering approached, he felt uneasy without knowing why. On my couch, he did not speak about the birthday party. He did not report it since it did not come to his mind. But I knew that he had put a new advertisement in a national journal seeking a woman and that he had already received many responses. For some months, he had given up advertising for a woman "to keep company with an active grandfather." I did not know his reason for returning to this "solution" for finding his idealized mother/Abigail. Therefore, I waited to see what would develop and what I would hear as a possible reason for his returning to this symptom.

After a Friday session with me, he had an urge to fly to a distant city to meet with a well-known television soap opera actress, one of the respondents to his recent advertisement. She had also sent him a picture in which she looked like Hamilton's young mother as she was in her thirties. The birthday gathering would take place on Sunday afternoon and Hamilton felt he had to see the television actress before the party. He had lost his "insight," that by being with the actress he was symbolically seeking to be his mother's only darling before he could face his siblings' births (the birthday party). When he arrived in the distant city after a long airplane ride and met the actress, right away he felt cheated. In reality, the actress was in her fifties and did not resemble his young mother. Hamilton felt extremely disappointed and depressed. He was losing his mother in her thirties once more!

Since he was a "gentleman" and had promised the actress that he would entertain her, he took the woman to a fancy restaurant, pasted a smile on his face, and remained very polite. He felt that he did not need to make love to this woman and returned to his hotel room alone, where he experienced further agitation and depression. The only way he could get rid of his troubled mood was to think of a quick solution. He remembered that another woman in the same city had responded to his advertisement. Finding her telephone number, he called her late at night, and made an arrangement to meet her for breakfast the next morning. Only then could he fall asleep.

The next morning he was pleased that his new date was indeed in her thirties. He quickly idealized her and they began spending time in bed. This woman warned Hamilton that she had recently been involved with a man in the high-risk category for AIDS. But, for Hamilton, the crucial psychological need was to possess this woman. The real physical danger of catching AIDS was secondary. Accordingly, he made love to her without using condoms, once more blurring his reality testing function.

Psychologically speaking, it was crucial for him to be "loved" by this woman, rather than participate in the "birthday event" (this was the phrase he used) that would take place in Richmond. I thought that if the "birthday event" did not take place, his "killing" his younger siblings in his unconscious fantasy would be true! Accordingly, he almost missed his flight home, but managed to make it to the "birthday event" on time. In the plane on his way back, he was surprised that he could not remember the name of the woman to whom he was making love some hours earlier. A thought came to his mind: "Okay, her name is 'pussy pill.'" This was another evidence that he was using his women representing "good" Abigail/ mother interchangeably. He managed to be amused as well as astonished by what he had done. He then realized that he had not told me about the "birthday event" and I did not know about his frantic flight to a distant city to find an idealized woman. Interestingly, he also sensed he could now present this repetition of behavior to me so that we could examine it together.

On Monday, during his first session following these events, Hamilton was thoughtful and analytical, assuring himself that he would not repeat such behavior again. He remembered how the separation from me during the last Labor Day holiday was so difficult because the word "labor" also refers to delivering babies.

Not long after this, Hamilton made some efforts to discover what had happened to the real Abigail and her brother, Morris. I approved. It was good for him to test his reality, learn about real people, instead of continually seeking their mental representations in others in order to find "solutions" for his internal conflicts. He made calls to people who might know about Abigail's life and whereabouts, but he could not gather a great deal of information. He learned that Abigail, who had died some years earlier, had lived all her life near Williamsburg, not far from Hamilton's original family home. He could not find out if she was ever married, if she had children and, if so, how many. He wondered if Abigail actually delivered a baby after she was fired from Hamilton's house because she was pregnant. Hamilton had no memories of Morris after Abigail was gone, but he did learn that Morris continued to work for Hamilton's family for years after his sister was fired.

Hamilton also let go of his first wife's ashes after a religious ceremony. The ashes were then buried in a churchyard. He had kept Della's ashes for eighteen years. He began to understand that he had not known how to mourn, how to let go of his "needed" companion. He was making an effort to learn. He referred to a childhood memory, which he had told me earlier. In the memory he was a small boy standing with his mother at an ice-cream stand. He wanted an ice-cream cone and his mother refused to buy it for him, so he had a temper-tantrum. I always thought that this memory summarized his rage when he "lost" his mother's breast (ice-cream cone) to his younger siblings. In the memory, he could still express his rage openly. Later, he had become an "obedient" boy, a "sissy" boy, and he could no longer express his rage openly nor could he learn how to let go of something that was lost.

He told me that his mother and/or Dolly had a habit of reporting Hamilton's and his older brother's misbehavior to the children's father when the older man returned home at night after working on the farm. Such complaints would lead to his father taking the boys to the "torture chamber." His father would pull Hamilton's pants down and beat the boy's buttocks with his razor strap. Child Hamilton's experiences in the "torture chamber"—in reality a big bathroom with a toilet in it—explains a great deal of adult Hamilton's preoccupation with what psychoanalysts call "anality," which he would soon bring to his analysis.

Since Sigmund Freud, psychoanalysts have observed developmental phases of childhood, each with its specific characteristics and psychological tasks.

VOLKAN: Freud was focusing on the internal world of the individual. His version of childhood developmental phases reflects elements coming from the child's internal world, mostly elements developing parallel to the importance of bodily sensations at different childhood epochs and the mental activities related to them: oral, anal, phallic, and genital (Oedipal) phases. After analysts became more aware of the role of the child's interaction with his or her environment (in early years dyadic mother-child relationships) in the development of the child's mind, new developmental phases were formulated referring to such relationships. For example, Mahler (1968) described autistic, symbiotic, and Oedipal phases with their subdivisions. Later when focus turned to the child's developing a self representation and his or her internalization of object representations and the interaction between various self and object images the developmental ladder was examined from still another point of view called object relations (Jacobson, 1964; Kernberg, 1976, 1980; Volkan, 1976). To look at the child development from a newer way does not or should not decrease the long-tested value of Freud's findings. The main stream of psychoanalysis "absorbs" new findings about human nature, but does not throw away previously tested and still valuable elements. Here in my description of Hamilton's difficulties I focus on his "anality." Obviously, I am also reporting the role of his childhood interpersonal relationships and more importantly the internalized versions of such relationships. I hope that the newcomers to our profession do not throw away the

Freudian forerunners to modern psychoanalytic theories—this is the equivalent of throwing the baby out with the bathwater. That would be a sad situation.

In our adult lives, under certain circumstances, we all often visit our developmental phases and utilize mental mechanisms associated with them. For example, when facing a stressful life event, a person may utilize oral mechanisms, and search for a nurturing person for solace or "spit out" unpleasant feelings and thoughts, and develop an illusion that such feelings or thoughts belong to someone else. Watching an athletic event may bring to our minds a phallic wish that our arm or leg muscles were as big as famous athletes' muscles. We also "compete" with others in various ways—hopefully harmless ways—for the attention of people of the opposite sex whom we find attractive. But some people, like Hamilton, become fixated with utilizing the defense mechanisms associated with the anal phase of development. He used excessively anal control mechanisms as if he were a prisoner in a mental bathroom, forever controlling his mental sphincter in order to protect his individuality and his relationships with others.

Little Hamilton was disappointed with his depressed mother. I thought that as a small child he reached up to the next level, the anal level, in order to escape his rage at losing his mother's breast. When little Hamilton was an Oedipal level child, he faced a father, who in reality was a punisher, a more than symbolic "castrator." So he reached back to the previous anal level, since staying at a phallic level and having a metaphorical sword fight with his scary father would be too terrifying. Thus, little Hamilton had created an anal level "mental" prison for himself and became a master, if you will, utilizing defense mechanisms that originally became prominent at the anal level of life; for example: intellectualization (explaining things away without experiencing such events' impact on his life), reaction formation (smiling while angry), isolation (not having emotions while thinking of the horror of the "torture chamber"), and ritualization (many of Hamilton's rituals have already been described). In short, Hamilton's mastering and excessive utilization of the so-called anal defense mechanisms allowed him to control his relationship with his own images as well as other people's images. Paradoxically, I think this mastery allowed him to have a life-long "adaptation" to his borderline personality organization. He could control his "good" and "bad" images and similar images of others, and hide his inner severe personality problems from those who only knew his public persona.

After allowing himself to experience that separations are real (his dead wife's ashes would not bring her to life again), Hamilton began to bring his anal stories to his sessions. In time I would learn how his childhood mailbox covered with the skirt of the woman teacher was not only his mother's womb, but also stood for a belly full of feces. The little boy secretly hidden in this woman's "belly" in fantasy could hurt the woman, or at least, in reality, scare the woman. So the little boy controlled himself as if he were the feces itself and did not "move." He controlled his rage. I would also learn how my couch, in his transference relationship to me, had become a bathroom. Hamilton recalled that when he was a little boy, Dolly instructed him to produce feces that were "firm, formed, but soft." As an adult, he knew that Dolly's orders were biologically improbable, but as a child he was made to think that he was a disobedient boy if his bowel movements did not fit her specifications. He perceived the retention (constipation) of the fecal material and the production of loose stools as causes for rejection by adults.

When he was in Abigail's kitchen and when Morris cleaned his bottom, no one cared about the quality or the quantity of his bowel movement. In fact, many chickens on the farm would gather around the kitchen and the houses where black servants lived, producing "inky messes," i.e., chicken droppings that were loose. In his mind, little Hamilton could not integrate "inky messes" with "firm, formed, but soft" stools. He could not integrate the mothering experiences he received from Abigail and other black servants with the mothering experiences he was exposed to in the big house. He recalled that he had a childhood phobia about stepping on chicken droppings. Adult Hamilton would feel very offended if another person used a "dirty" word in his presence. But he also enjoyed going to the run-down diner and recalling his childhood experiences in the black servants' kitchen where black people, men and women, gathered around a big stove and talked about "dirty" and sexy things. He could not really escape "inky" things. He then realized that not only in his social life, but also in his business life, he created "inky" messes and one of the reasons for his frequent trips to court was in the service of cleaning up such messes.

We were two years and three months into his analysis and Christmas was approaching when he became preoccupied with his list of one hundred women's names in his address book. He kept wondering to whom he should send gifts. He used a great deal of intellectualization to figure out why this woman should receive a gift this Christmas and why that woman should be deprived of one. He had some understanding that through "gifts" he was buying "pussy pills," and acknowledged that this purchase was really "fake love." At this phase of his analysis he was less aware that gifts or money stood for his feces. He was going to give his feces to others (representing Dolly and his parents) and find out who would appreciate his anal productions.

If his gifts were "firm, formed and soft," he would be loved. If they were not, he would be rejected. Once more, he recalled taking a very expensive bouquet of flowers to a woman who angrily threw his gift back at him at the door of her house, soiling the nice suit he was wearing. He gave a lottery ticket to the man and woman who owned the run-down diner in hopes that they might experience a "big surprise" and have a great deal of money to enjoy (have many "inky messes" in their surroundings). Meanwhile, in order psychologically to balance this "generosity," he "forgot" the amount of my fee. He demanded that I tell him how much I was charging him per session. I gave no response and waited for the story to evolve and ripen. Of course, by looking at his bank account, he could easily "remember" the amount. But, instead of doing so, he came to his next hour once more demanding that I tell him the amount of my fee.

VOLKAN: He forgets the fee, and then asks me to tell him what I charge—after two years of analysis! I do not respond because this is his unconscious hostility coming forth in the room with me. He is frustrating me but I do not tell him. My sense of frustration disappears when I sense that he is going to repeat in the transference what had happened between him and childhood objects that demanded that he has "perfect" feces. If I speak I may interfere with the mounting transference expectations and affects related to them. I do not tell him the fee. Often, not saying anything is as important to the growing transference as is making a profound interpretation.

FOWLER: At this moment he asks you the fee and you don't say. The next day he loudly insists you tell him the fee. Still, you say nothing. Why?

VOLKAN: By his next session, his demand became louder, accompanied by anxiety. This time, instead of telling him the amount of my fee, I told him that he was making me like Dolly, wanting to know what kind of feces I wanted him to produce (I deliberately used the "forbidden" word "shit"). He laughed, indicating that he understood what I said.

VOLKAN: A better question would be, "Why does Hamilton tolerate my silent refusal?" He knows that I will speak when it will be useful for both of us. He knows that my silence is out of respect for him, to protect the analytic process, and help him experience something new. The therapeutic alliance makes it possible for him to tolerate my silence.

FOWLER: So, when you do not speak, you are inviting this angry, hidden part of his personality into the analysis?

VOLKAN: The major therapeutic action in psychoanalysis is for Hamilton to bring his internal world, his affects, defenses, and adaptations between us so we can "touch" them. Once this is done he will attempt to work through the conflicts in a new way and resolve them. If I give him a logical answer, I break the psychoanalytic frame and one of my key rules is gone. This rule is that I am not managing his social life.

FOWLER: Some psychoanalysts would say that this is not presenting Hamilton with a human response. They would argue that the analyst should provide Hamilton with an "empathic" response by answering his question. How would you address this criticism?

VOLKAN: Obviously, there are situations in which you respond spontaneously and logically. In this situation I have empathy for his struggle to bring his anal conflict between us. And, it is because of my empathy for him that I do not answer his question. I do not spoil his hard transference work. This does not mean that "classical analysts" lack empathy. A psychoanalytic process cannot take place without the analyst's experience of empathy. Also what one person may think is an empathic response may not register as empathic reaction by the patient. I have an example of this from a case I supervised. A man comes in to ses-

sion and tells the analyst that his daughter was just in a horrible car accident and was injured. If you came to me as a colleague and told me this same news, then my heart goes out to you, and I would say, "Dr. Fowler, I am so sorry to hear that!" The analyst I supervised said to that patient, "I'm sorry to hear about your daughter," and immediately the patient became furious. He screamed, "I am quitting analysis. You have no understanding of how I feel! What kind of person are you?" The analyst gave what appeared to be an empathic response, but the result was the patient became infuriated! The analyst came to me and reported this event. I knew that the patient was a very narcissistic man. He had just made a multi-million dollar deal to develop deadly weapons for the US government. The man was furious because his daughter's accident had spoiled his great day. And how dare his analyst not understand that his fantastic accomplishment was ruined! So, what might have been a fitting empathic response that reaches this patient's internal world? The analyst might say, "How terrible that your daughter's accident spoiled this glorious time in your life." This is a deeply selfish sentiment, but the patient had not worked through his extreme narcissism. In two or three more years in analysis, he could have experienced a socially acceptable reaction to his daughter's accident, but not at that moment.

That night Hamilton had a dream and brought it to his next day's session:

> I entered a bathroom and saw a fat man with your (analyst's) skin color, sitting on a commode. There was no wall or other enclosure around the commode. This reminded me of a child sitting on a potty in the middle of a big living room. Everyone in the room could see the boy sitting on a potty. The fat man in fact looked like a balloon, blown up, bloated. Watching this man, in the dream, I felt very anxious, and I woke up.

With little help from me, Hamilton realized that the fat man in the dream represented his own belly filled with feces. In the dream, he had projected his constipated and ready-to-explode self onto the analyst. He was keeping his feces inside because he did not know if Dolly/analyst would like the appearance of his stool. (This is why he forgot the amount of my fee and kept asking me to tell him how much it was; to describe to him what kind of feces I wanted him to produce.) By keeping his feces inside, he was also depriving Dolly/analyst of his production, and thus he was expressing his anger through constipation. But, the feces that were accumulated in his belly could explode. Thus, he projected the exploding feces-full belly onto the analyst's image. In reality, Hamilton has very fair skin and my skin color is darker than his. At times, in his mind, I also stood for the African-Americans of his childhood.

As he was making an association with the fat man dream, Hamilton suddenly recalled the first dream he had brought to his analysis: a black man hanging by a rope. Now, I could interpret for Hamilton the meaning of the black man with a tight rope around his neck. The rope represented his anal sphincter and the dream reflected his control of his sphincter. To produce or not produce his feces was under his control. His first dream in analysis therefore was a symbolic expression of his resistance to analysis. Just as he had "controlled" all other personal relationships, he wanted to "control" his analyst, too.

Hamilton continued his session informing me that, on the way to the session, he had suddenly remembered the amount of my fee, and proceeded to report that he no longer wanted to pay money to Mary every month. There was still no court decision about this matter however, so he was obliged to continue to produce "feces" for Mary.

Hamilton returned to his fat man dream and gave further associations to it. He had been reading a book about the life of Alfred Nobel. He made a slip of the tongue and instead of "Nobel" he used the word "Noble." Knowing that Nobel was the "discoverer" and manufacturer of dynamite, I thought that Hamilton was preparing to sense and speak about his anal sadism, which is usually symbolized as an explosion. "Noble" stood for his FFV ancestors. He was condensing his ancestors into the image of a man who could produce explosions. Hamilton himself was a "noble" who could also blast others to pieces.

Hamilton told me how Alfred Nobel lived with a young woman who became pregnant by someone else and married this individual. Nevertheless, Nobel continued to support her. I caught an echo in this story of Abigail's pregnancy and her leaving him. He had a wish that his "noble" parents had not dismissed his beloved nanny.

During the remainder of the session, he went into detail about how to make dynamite and how to explode it. As he spoke, he was very animated, moving his arms and legs. I listened to him silently and then said: "Are we getting ready to see the fat man on the commode explode?" He replied: "Oh! Yes! This morning, after having my dream, I woke up constipated." After waking up, he explained he had to uncharacteristically rush to the bathroom and strained to move his bowels. As he was telling me this, his voice dropped to a whisper and he reported that the feces that came out of him were very "hard." I told him that he might be afraid that I, like Dolly, would not accept a "hard" stool, and that he would not be loved, and that I might retaliate against him and hurt him because of his "hard shit." He said that he had an excuse, and added: "I was tense yesterday during our session. Tension causes hard bowel movements."

He regressed further on my couch and appeared as if he had gone into a trance-like state. I did not interfere. After five minutes or so, when he came out of it, he said that he was recalling how his mother had taught him how to fold toilet tissue in order to wipe off his bottom without touching the fecal material. His mother insisted that only soft toilet paper be used. "It would feel nice on one's bottom." I explained how confusing this might be to him since, by complaining about his behavior, his mother would initiate his father's beating his son's bottom with a hard razor strap. I said I understood how difficult it was to think of his mother as one and the same person when, one moment she was kindly encouraging him to gently wipe his bottom, and the next moment she was the instigator of severe punishment. I also told him how difficult it was for him to live both with "inky messes" loving black people and "inky messes" hating white people, during his childhood years.

The next day he told me that grandmother Dolly's childrearing practices included giving enemas to children. He suddenly remembered that his father and mother also took enemas. He was sure that there were enema tubes of different sizes on the shelf in the big bathroom in their second farmhouse. It should be recalled that this room had been a library. Books were gone and shelves were filled with enema tubes, jars of laxatives, and mineral oils. As a child, he had to take a teaspoonful of mineral oil. Occasionally, he was given a seed of a fruit—he could not recall the name—as a laxative. He also knew about "high colonic irrigation" practices, which were part of his family's routine. Yet, he could not bring himself to utter the word "shit." Only black people could talk like that and be surrounded by "inky messes." They, and those, like little Hamilton, who loved the black individuals openly or secretly, were degraded by his "noble," white family members.

FOWLER: This sequence is intriguing. Hamilton is experiencing you as a split representation of his parents in the sessions and represented in the dream—noble, caring, and then disconnected from that experience as dangerous and harsh. His dream of constipation and the symbolic explosive anger seem to consolidate in the sessions with you as you "invite" the transference to deepen. Then you interpret the difficulty you know he must have in comprehending his parents in these opposite ways. How do you help Hamilton mend these opposing images?

VOLKAN: He is effectively sensing both sides . . .not integrated yet, he's sensing them. When he came in during the first two years, he told me his story as if he were reading a newspaper to me. This dream and his associations were full of feeling and imagery. He connects actual constipation with his dream and he connects it with Alfred Nobel and explosions. He connects the symbols, and then he remembers his tension, his bowel movement. This session is not like listening to him read a newspaper. His body knows it. He sees symbolism in himself, coming up in dreams, so things are changing. Every child goes through a routine, a "normal" phase of being unable to integrate his or her self and object images. There is such a thing that can be called a "developmental splitting" in the normal development (Jacobson, 1964; Kernberg, 1976, 1980; Volkan, 1976, 1981). If everything goes well without mental complication the child, developmentally speaking, mends his or her split self and object images. If complications occur, as they did in little Hamilton's case, the normal "developmental splitting" remains and turns into a "defensive splitting." The child uses this defense, as Hamilton did, to stay away from tensions and conflict of bringing together "good" and "bad" images. Once in analysis, the splitting (of course the defensive one) appears in the patient's history, in the everyday life, in dreams, and in the transference. After the patient has enough experience sensing how and why he or she uses a defensive splitting, in a state of a therapeutic regression the "developmental splitting" reappears and the patient comes under the influence of a "developmental push" (like a normal child would have) to mend his self and object images. In the following chapters we will see how I will help Hamilton with his "developmental push" to mend his self and object images.

Chapter 4
Pineapple Upside-Down Cake

Hamilton's dream about a fat man on a commode was reported as Christmas approached and we had one more week before we would separate for the holidays. Here, I will report what happened during this week and when we resumed our work after the holidays. The events will illustrate clearly how an analysand in a therapeutic regression creates a therapeutic play and drastically works through some of his or her internal conflicts. By the term "therapeutic play," I am referring to an analysand's involvement in an action that is carried out for many days or weeks accompanied by a story in the service of remembering and attempting to master a childhood conflict. The image of the analysand as a child is involved in the play. Also, the corresponding image of the analyst as a transference figure (representing, for example, a parent image involved in the analysand's conflict) also appears in the story, as does a "new object" (representing a new image of the same parent figure who this time helps the analysand to respond to his or her conflict in a more adaptive way). When the action and the accompanying story comes to an end, the analysand experientially "learns" to expect a different response from "others" to his or her conflict, and in turn, to give a more adaptive response to his or her internal pressure. The action in a therapeutic play is not a resistance to the analysis. In fact, it constitutes a major part of the patient's working through his or her conflict. The analysand, of course, may recreate his or her conflict in the future during analytic sessions for a second, third, and fourth look at it. But, the drastic examination of the conflict through a therapeutic play involving the patient and the analyst has its own specific place in the therapeutic process. At this point, the analysand is like a sculptor who finally finishes his or her sculpture, a work that induces a sense of accomplishment in him or her. Subsequent work on the sculpture serves to polish and refine it, which itself takes time and is necessary for the final product.

FOWLER: Given the importance of the therapeutic play, will you expand on the concept and its place in psychoanalytic treatment?

VOLKAN: I have written about the therapeutic play elsewhere (Volkan, 1984) as a special aspect of transference neurosis. A neurotic individual who is capable of utilizing symbols and has no particular difficulty in reality testing (or a borderline or narcissistic individual who through treatment begins to function like a neurotic person) creates a therapeutic play after the resolution of a specific aspect of the transference neurosis has begun—largely, in fact, after it has taken place and there is less unconscious resistance to its development. The play, accompanied by actions, develops from session to session for weeks, sometimes even months, as a way of recapturing a crucial aspect of the transference neurosis, of which the patient is conscious and which the patient has already substantially resolved. Consider, for instance, a neurotic man who, as a young child, lost his father and subsequently developed the unconscious fantasy that he was his father's "killer": Three and a half years into his analysis, after the transference neurosis pertaining to his unconscious fantasy has been interpreted and mostly worked through, this adult patient lives out a drama about the potential threats to the analyst's life. The patient checks the tires of the analyst's car parked in front of his office, declares that the tires are worn, and warns that the analyst may have a fatal accident. Since "killing" the analyst has become a very familiar story by this point, and since the analyst and the patient both know its meaning, the analyst does not probe it. By the next session, the patient has checked the electrical wires in the analyst's building with the same idea: that the analyst may meet his death in an accident, this time by fire. The analyst again remains silent. During the following sessions, the analysand fully develops a "story" of how the analyst will die: he talks about nothing else, and, after several weeks, the "story" comes to a point at which the patient perceives the analyst as seriously ill and on the verge of death. Meanwhile, the patient experiences various emotions about "killing" his analyst. Finally, one session, the analysand suddenly begins to laugh with relief: "You know," he says, "I have been trying to kill you. I knew all along what I have been doing. But you are still alive! I now surely know that I did not kill my father. Now I feel free of guilt." There is nothing for the analyst to interpret; he offers only his affirmative "Hm! Hm!" and soon the patient enters the termination phase of his analysis.

As in this example, therapeutic play typically includes action in which the images of both patient and analyst are prominent. These actions, such as this patient's tire-checking, ultimately help the patient to master the resolution of the transference neurosis and thus do not fall into the category of "acting out" (Freud, 1914), as a way of maintaining repression. Rather, the actions associated with a therapeutic play help to crystallize the working-through of the patient's major mental conflicts and thus to render harmless associated unconscious fantasies' pathogenic influence (see also Blum, 1976; Boesky, 1982). Some of these actions may take place outside the analyst's office and outside of sessions, but mostly they are confined to the analyst's office; when the play comes freely to an end and is finally verbalized, the patient's actions cease.

I will now describe the events within and outside of my office that took place during the week before the Christmas vacation as well as what happened when we met again after the Christmas vacation. I describe my interactions with Hamilton during these times in great detail in order to illustrate the nature of a therapeutic play concerning his anal conflicts, my response to them, and Hamilton's resolution of his anal as well as phallic conflicts.

On Monday, while driving to my office for his session, Hamilton tried to drink orange juice from a bottle and "by accident" spilled the juice on his pants. Thus, after he parked his bright yellow car in front of my office in the red brick house at Blue Ridge Hospital, he rushed to the bathroom to clean the spots caused by his spilling the orange juice. But again, "by accident" he made a "mess" and the wetness on his pants spread all over. When he came to my room, he was wearing his overcoat. He appeared very reluctant to take off his coat and lie on my couch. I made no remarks and patiently waited. He said that his pants were wet. He added that he would be extremely embarrassed to exhibit his wet pants in front of me. I was puzzled, but said nothing. He took off his overcoat, hung it on a coat hanger at one corner of my room, quickly took his place on the couch and reported how he had two "accidents." (The phrase "having an accident" also refers to soiling one's pants.) I made some "Hm! Hm!" sounds, indicating that I was carefully listening to him. He then reported that there had been a Christmas gathering over the weekend at his brother's house. When he went there, he noted that Dorothy, on whose legs he had ejaculated when they were both young, was there also. She had come from her home in Georgia to Richmond in order to join this family gathering. Hamilton told me how uncomfortable he had felt. He also appeared very uncomfortable on the couch. I thought that by wetting his pants, Hamilton symbolically connected his feces and urine with his semen and brought his bodily products to his analyst in order to dramatically repeat his childhood experiences in analysis. Since his story was not yet fully revealed, I remained silent and listened to him.

Next he reported that recently some new people had rented the house across from his brother's house. During the family Christmas gathering, he heard his brother speak of his new neighbors, saying that they were strange people because they stayed in their new house only occasionally. Upon hearing this, Hamilton began to imagine that these strange people might be "terrorists" and "bomb makers" who were using the place as a "safe house."

I told Hamilton that his thoughts about "bomb makers" might be connected with the fat man on the commode who might have an anal explosion and whom he had dreamed about during the previous week. I interpreted my understanding of what he was exhibiting and telling me during the initial part of the session: I told Hamilton that his feelings about the upcoming birthday of a child (Jesus Christ) at Christmas and the separation from me (mother) had caused him discomfort.

VOLKAN: Bryce Boyer (1983) examined seventeen cases of serious depressions that emerged during the Christian holiday celebrating the birth of Jesus Christ. Boyer contends that these depressive episodes are, in part, evoked by rekindled sibling rivalries. The symbolic golden child, so favored and adored by Christians, cannot possibly be competed with. Regressed patients who felt pushed from the status of the beloved baby when a sibling was born are prone to experiencing such depressions. Hamilton's sibling rivalries and his constant search for the perfect woman brought this to mind and helped me formulate this interpretation.

I added that through our work together he was mindful of the connection between his anxiety and younger siblings' births and separations. This time, however, he might be recalling an additional event that had induced anxiety in him: squirting "bullets" (sperm) on his sister's body. I also reminded him that once he had told me how, by wetting his bed, he would fantasize he was protecting himself from possible homosexual attacks by his brother with whom he had to share a bed. His brother would move away from him in order not to touch Hamilton's urine. By coming to his session with wet pants perhaps he thought we might look into the issues I just mentioned. I added that his hesitation to show me his "mess" and "sperm" might also be due to his expectation that I would react like Dolly, his parents, or his brother. If he were ready, I said to him, we could become curious together, to see what would develop between us next. "Let your mind wander," I suggested.

FOWLER: Hamilton's "accident" appears to be the work of his unconscious to bring his "inky messes" to you. I thought your statement to him was a clear example of linking the internal representations with you as a transference object. Once you made the connections to his internal objects and the dream image of the fat man on the commode, you then invited him to become curious with you to see what would develop between the two of you.

VOLKAN: I am setting the groundwork for Hamilton's working through his conflicts and I am making an indirect reference to therapeutic alliance. Hamilton is making his unconscious conflicts come to life in my presence. I am telling him I understand some of the symbolic meanings and links, but I am also learning with him the things he does not yet know. I cannot interpret the story before it happens! We must first let the story unfold. In this session, he did not actually urinate or ejaculate; he created a yellow looking wet stain on the crotch of his pants. Because he is in a therapeutic regression, his childhood fears are reawakened with me as the one who may punish, attack, or seduce him. He is now having a repetition compulsion in the analysis in an intense way in front of me whereas before he only had repetition compulsion in life outside the analysis at the diner, with his women, and with other business associates. Now he begins testing out the possibility that he can work through such fears with me present. This is a very important part of psychoanalytic practice—when patients live out the repetition compulsion in the analysis, the analyst may help them create a new and different ending. So he is going to have a different ending with me in the transference; and that is going to be settling in him so he will not get anxious when he thinks he has made a mess. So, it is part of working through. I say a couple of words to encourage him to work with me. If, at the end of this process, he comes to the realization and he says, "Oh my God. I repeated this with you and I was not punished or castrated! I can play with messes," then I can make my interpretation, or simply acknowledge my agreement with his conclusions with a hearty, "Hm, Hm!

Hamilton began speaking about a new experiment he was carrying out. Some months earlier, he was introduced to Michelle, a divorced woman of Belgian (blonde and light-skinned) origin. Michelle was a beautiful refined lady in her early forties who spoke six languages. Hamilton gave up dating other women and wanted to have Michelle as his steady girlfriend. Without telling me first, he was "experimenting" by being with Michelle for two consecutive nights. The week before, in fact, he had bravely spent three consecutive nights with Michelle without turning her into a "devil."

The night before this Monday morning session, he had been with Michelle. When he woke up, he noticed a wet spot on the bed sheet caused by the couple's sexual activity. When he got into the car to come to see me, he was worried that the cleaning lady, who would come to the apartment that day, might notice the sex-related spot and consider him "dirty." Then he had his "accident" by spilling the orange juice on his pants and by making a "bigger mess" in my bathroom. He agreed that by "wetting" his pants, he brought his sexualized "inky mess" to my office and symbolically put it between us so that I would stay away like his brother had stayed away from him while sharing the bed. Thus, Hamilton was protecting himself from my (homosexual) assault.

Hamilton and I regularly met on Mondays, Wednesdays, Thursdays and Fridays. Accordingly, we had no sessions on Tuesday following the incident of his "wetting" his pants. Recently Hamilton had begun to have "afternoon delights" with Michelle on Tuesdays. I always "heard" his reference to "afternoon delights" as "Turkish delights," the common name of certain Turkish candy. Thus I thought, in a way Michele also represented me, the Turkish analyst. Hamilton was working on decreasing his splitting of a woman's image with me "out there." Because I sensed that this type of "ego activity" would be useful to him, I made no remarks about the idea that Michelle might be connected with his transference toward me. An analyst chooses when to make an interpretation and when not to make one.

FOWLER: He has begun a "new relationship with a woman named Michelle." On Tuesday on the day he doesn't see you, he has started to have what he calls "Afternoon Delights" that you then call Turkish Delights.

VOLKAN: As it is clear to the reader, I am a Turkish American. Turkish Delights is absolutely my fantasy creation. I am creatively placing myself in the mental world of Hamilton in order to understand what he may be doing with me. I did not tell him this, I did not ask him to free associate to the phrase, "afternoon delights." It is my way of joining his internal world.

FOWLER: What is so interesting is that you did not simply accept the external reality of Michelle as a "new object" with whom Hamilton can work through conflicts. Rather, you mentally placed yourself as the new object and viewed Michelle as a figure on whom Hamilton could displace the transference.

VOLKAN: In a sense Michelle is me, and is not me. I am not a woman—I am not his mother either. He is looking for another idealized mother. Until recently he has always split the good image of mother from the bad image. Hamilton could not tolerate spending a night with the same woman two nights on a row because she, the "good" one, always turned into a "devil" on the second day. Hamilton is experimenting with his internal world by spending two nights in a row with Michele. What he is doing is very different. It is called an "ego exercise" for gaining new ego functions, in this case mending the opposite images of an intimate object. I do not interfere with my "interpretations."

FOWLER: I notice that you do not relinquish the transference meaning by focusing on Michelle as a person that is good for Hamilton. I can imagine that some therapists would want to know more about Michelle as a real person, as opposed to how Hamilton is working on internal images.
VOLKAN: I am in the room with Hamilton to help him to do analytic work. I am not there to be a parent or teacher or friend who congratulates him whenever he does well. Doing this would infantilize him or treat him like a good student of proper personal relationships. Having said this, sometimes I do feel delighted and happy to see Hamilton's progress and his new ability to effectively use a new ego function. If he senses my delight correctly then I do not deny how I feel because the "denial" of my feeling at this time will be my being disrespectful of his reality testing.

Before he came to his second session that week on Wednesday, Hamilton had another "afternoon delight." I thought symbolically he was with me (the Turkish analyst) and in the transference I was his beloved Abigail or his mother's beautiful "titties." Hidden beneath this understanding was his fear that being with the "Turkish" analyst would make him a homosexual whenever I would become a male in his mind.

On Wednesday he reported how the day before he imagined Michelle not to be a nice person. While they were together, he saw his "bad" mother in her and recalled his mother's whipping him. Next he spoke of a childhood memory of how puppies were trained: "You push the puppy's nose into his feces when the puppy makes a mess in the house, and hit him with a newspaper."

I remained silent and refrained from immediately telling him that I thought the puppy stood for little Hamilton. I wanted him to experience little Hamilton's emotions. Then he reported what came to his mind next: "When I was a small child one of my cousins and I had a special game. We would pretend we were putting an enema tube into a black woman's anus and blowing her up." Then he became very anxious, unable to speak and appeared paralyzed with fear. After waiting a few minutes for him to relive the impact of his anxiety, I told him that he might wish to give an enema to Michelle and explode her. I added that while he was able to have "afternoon delights" with Michelle and experiment to sleep with her two nights in a row she, like his other many previous women, could still, in his mind, turn to be "bad." I said: "No wonder your childhood image blowing up a woman, Abigail who rejected you, has come to your mind." He murmured: "Sweet revenge!" But then he felt paralyzed again.

After awhile, he began to speak of a businessman of Turkish origin in Richmond. Hamilton had met him recently and this "Turk" was modest and polite. In the past I had met this man who is older than both of us. I did not tell Hamilton I knew this man, but I knew Hamilton's perception of him was correct. This time I chose to tell Hamilton that this "Turk" represented me. I told Hamilton that he was changing me into a gentle Turk because he was still afraid of rejections, beatings, homosexual attacks, and torture if he experienced his childhood rage, "like blowing up a woman through putting an enema tube into her anus." I asked him if he could tolerate imagining that he not only wanted to urinate and defecate on me, but he wanted to put an enema tube into me and also use me as a target for his sperm bullets and "kill" me like he wanted to kill Dorothy, his rejecting mother, big brother who might approach him sexually in the bed they shared, and scary father in the "torture chamber." I wondered out loud what kind of guarantee he needed in order to express his negative thoughts and feelings openly without an expectation of punishment. Then I added that he might consider that such thoughts and feelings, which he could not tame when he was a child, might be dealt with playfully since he was now an adult. I also told Hamilton that I would tolerate such thoughts and feelings if he would.

FOWLER: In this session, Hamilton gets anxious after you wonder if he wanted to blow you up. Then you did something that I found curious. You wondered out loud what kind of guarantee he needed in order to express negative thoughts and feelings openly without an expectation of punishment.

VOLKAN: Well, for Hamilton it is an awful thing to think of aggressive things—you see he still cannot distinguish between feeling and fantasy on the one hand and reality and action on the other. It is a thin distinction for him. He fears actually harming me if he fantasizes about blowing me up. The infantile fantasies of childhood still frighten him. He was a grown man by the time he came to me, but because of his traumas and character formation, he repeats the same things again and again. Intellectually, he can say to himself that he is an adult, but his affective life is too frightening to him—it is too real. I was confident that I could tolerate his murderous rage because I was analyzed and I had been in the professional business of analyzing others for many years. One anxious person in this room is enough. As long as I am not anxious about his fantasies and feelings, I will remain in the role as his analyst. It is my job to protect the frame. I tell him it is like a play. I give him the freedom to play with his messes with me. As long as I don't introduce or create the play or force a storyline on him, he can create his own therapeutic stories or plays.

That afternoon on December 21, 1988, after our session, I heard the news that the New York bound PAN AM flight 103 exploded over Lockerbie, Scotland, killing 259 people aboard and eleven on the ground. When I heard the news, I thought of Hamilton. I wondered if the external tragedy might make him very anxious, and if he might connect the bomb that caused the PAN AM crash with his psychic "anal bomb." When he came to his Thursday session, the first thing he reported was that he brought me a Christmas gift. Immediately, I thought that indeed the tragedy at Lockerbie was unconsciously condensed within his wish to explode his "anal bomb." This scared him, I thought. Thus, he was going to be a good boy and bring me a "gift." He made no reference to the plane crash and, in turn, I did not bring the topic up in order to see how the story of his giving me a gift would evolve.

Until then, Hamilton had never brought up the notion of giving me a gift. As I stated, he started this Thursday session by telling me that he had brought me a gift, but he was carrying no packages. After lying on the couch, he reported that his gift for me was a pineapple upside-down cake. But, he had forgotten to bring the cake—in a gift-wrapped box—to my office and had left it on the back seat of his fancy sports car parked in front of the house where we had our sessions. In a most unusual gesture, he lifted his head up from the couch and looked through the window at the car, which could be seen parked outside. The gift was in the car. I thought that he wanted to satisfy me orally so that I would not punish him for his anal explosion. But I also knew that his gift was still contaminated with aggression and that was the reason why he could not bring it to my room, and that might be the reason why he wanted to see his car and be sure that it did not explode like the PAN AM airplane. Hamilton was anxious and I remained silent.

After settling down on the couch, he put his smile back on his face, appeared relaxed, and began to describe in minute detail the nature of his gift. He called it a pineapple "upside down" cake. I thought that "upside down" symbolically referred to his feces that would come out of his body. I also thought that his gift might refer to his two younger sisters whom he hated when he was a child, and who came out of their mother's body head first, "upside down." It occurred to me that he might wish to discard them from his environment like "a piece of shit," by giving them to me. But I also sensed his gift was simply his childhood feces contaminated with his aggression that would also protect him from being sexually assaulted by his brother. Hamilton told me that the cake was of a dark color. It also had raisins and nuts. When he said that the cake was "firm, formed, but soft," I reminded him that earlier he had described something else using the same adjectives. Upon hearing me, Hamilton burst into explosive laughter. "I can't help it!" he yelled. "I want your approval. I don't want to be punished!"

FOWLER: When Hamilton describes the cake to you as firm, formed and soft, you remind him that he described something else using the same adjectives. He explodes in laughter and says, "I want your approval. I don't want to be punished." How would you describe this action?

VOLKAN: He's reliving the scary interaction with Dolly and/mother. I am helping him to see it or play with its repetition of this event between us more openly. Obviously when I tell him his cake is a piece of feces, my words may be constructed as an interpretation. If Hamilton did not know consciously that his cake stood for his childhood feces I am giving him information and also telling him the name what his symbol represents. I am making something unconscious conscious and my interpretation has a direct relationship with the transference story.

FOWLER: Might we think of this as your recognition of your multiple meanings of this gift?

VOLKAN: He has been speaking and operating with a particular fascination about anal activities. But just as he starts to play around with these fantasies in the transference, an actual tragedy strikes in the real world—a bomb explodes, a plane falls down, and people are killed. If someone like Hamilton has murder-

ous rage and little capacity to differentiate fantasy from reality, he does not know if rage can harm others. As he is working on this a drastic dangerous thing happens in the external reality; he makes a connection between the external event and internal expectations. He stops his therapeutic play, and he regresses in a defensive retreat away from play and into trying to pacify me (this type of regression is not therapeutic because it is a retreat from the story and the playful engagement). When this type of event occurs, then I have to help Hamilton work his way back into the therapeutic play.

He went into an uncomfortable silence and I stayed silent too so I would not spoil his discomfort or interfere with the psychological process he was bringing to his session. My spoiling his uncomfortable silence would mean my disrespect for the hard work he was doing. My calming him down would mean my not having any empathy or trust in his developing ability to experience scary feelings. Then he described his hearing about the PAN AM plane crash just before going to a store to buy gifts, one for me and some for others (including some women from his address book). The saleslady was "nasty" to him and told him to wait in the store while she wrapped his gifts. She told him that if he did not stay in the store and wait, she would not help him or wrap his gifts. Hamilton reported to me that the saleslady's attitude or "orders" reminded him of his mother or Dolly telling him to sit on the potty and "wait" until he produced his "perfect" feces: "firm, formed, but soft." He wanted to please me, but he was afraid that his cake might not live up to my expectations. This was why he had "forgotten" to bring it into my office, he said.

Before the Thursday session was over, I told Hamilton that if I accepted his "perfect feces," we would bypass working on his feelings of submission to Dolly's orders against biology and his rage concerning adult intrusions into his body by using enema tubes. I asked him if he could put his thoughts and feelings about giving me a gift into words. He said that he understood the meaning of his gesture, but he still wanted to give me the cake as a Christmas gift. After all, a gift was a gift. As a Turk, he added, I might not have the custom of celebrating Christmas, but in his tradition, Christmas was a time to give gifts. He pasted his smile on his face and left my office.

The next day, Friday, again he came to my office without carrying a gift-wrapped box. After lying on my couch, he said nothing about the cake, but instead reported a dream. In the first part of the dream, two women were checking his urine to see if it contained sugar. He spontaneously interpreted this part of the dream: The two women stood for the idealized companions of his childhood, nurturing Abigail and/or his mother with beautiful "nanas," as well as for his "bad" rejecting Abigail and his rejecting mother who had turned her attention to his younger sisters. He said that, according to his perception of his women, they are either "good" or "bad." He himself, in a corresponding way, could have "sweet" urine or "aggressive" urine. "They were testing my feelings about them," he added, and reported the rest of the dream in which the testing of his urine took place in a room at the University of Virginia Hospital, which in reality is about five miles away from the Blue Ridge Hospital. The room was dark and had a "back entrance" through which railroad tracks came into the hospital (in reality no such back entrance exists). There was a big locomotive on the tracks and it went "in and out" of the room. Hamilton was aware of having great discomfort while dreaming.

As soon as he finished telling me the second part of the dream, Hamilton told me that before falling asleep he had sex with Michelle, but could not reach orgasm. He was upset about it. Sensing his frustration, Michelle told him: "You do not have to come!"

I told him that while having sex with Michelle he had a conflict over giving her his semen or retaining his semen. In the dream, I told him, the locomotive most likely stood for his feces. The locomotive could enter his body through the back door (anus) and stay inside the dark room (his belly) or the locomotive (feces) could go out of his body. The way Dolly and his mother treated him induced mixed feelings about producing or not producing feces for them. He was conflicted about wishing to please them and, at the same time, wishing to deprive them of his gift (feces). Upon hearing this, Hamilton told me that after our last session he had put the pineapple upside down cake in the trunk (backside) of his car and locked it in there. Before coming to my office for the Friday session, once more he had forgotten to bring the cake to me. But still, he wanted to give it to me.

When Hamilton reported his dream, I also noticed homosexual symbolism connected with the locomotive going "in and out" of his anus. The locomotive, I thought, could also stand for enema tubes and also for his father's/brother's phallus. If he did not please his mother, she would initiate punishment and his father would remove his pants and beat him with a razor strap on his buttocks, or his brother would (in fantasy) assault him in the bed they shared. I assumed that Hamilton had an unconscious fantasy of sexual assault when he was given enemas and/or when he was beaten on his buttocks. Since the event in the dream took place at the main University of Virginia Hospital where I taught, Hamilton was including my image in his dream. But, by dreaming about the main University of Virginia Hospital instead of the Blue Ridge Hospital, he was also putting some distance (isolation) between the anxiety-provoking events and feelings about me as a transference figure representing dangerous people of his childhood.

The manifest content of any dream, when examined closely, reveals multiple meanings that are condensed within one another. The task of the analyst is not to tell the patient every possible meaning the manifest content of the dream might have, but to focus on what is "hot," and consider what interpretation will help with further development of the primary therapeutic story. His primary therapeutic story, I sensed, focused on pleasing or not pleasing his mother and Dolly and the symbolic power of his "inky messes." If he exploded his feces, he could kill! Then I (father/brother) would not be able to sexually assault him as punishment.

In talking to Hamilton, I thought that I should stay primarily with the anal aspect of his dream, but not bring to his attention too quickly the idea that he might sexualize in his mind analyst/father/brother's assault on him as a punishment for his angry feelings. While I was wondering if he was ready to explore his sexualized fantasies, Hamilton himself brought his father's image to the therapeutic story that was being reenacted between us, and referred to his anxiety about homosexual submission to his father/me.

His reference to homosexual submission appeared in a second dream that Hamilton reported during the same session. In this dream a "foreigner" comes to Hamilton's house. (He knew that this "foreigner" stood for his analyst, since I am an immigrant to the USA and speak English with a Turkish accent.) In the dream, the foreigner and Hamilton are involved in doing something together. Hamilton thought they went to a school together. (I thought that doing something together represented our collaboration in analyzing him.) The foreigner wanted a shirt and Hamilton took off his shirt and gave it to the foreigner. When Hamilton searched for another one to wear, all he could find was a blue shirt with a checkered design, so he put it on. At this time, an unusual thing happened. The foreigner was no longer wearing Hamilton's shirt, but was wearing a Nazi uniform and a Nazi hat. He had turned into a Nazi officer. While Hamilton's family was in no way connected to the Jewish holocaust, the impact of such horrific imagery resonated with his internal life of destructive objects. It is remarkably common for people who are not Jewish to incorporate such widely publicized atrocities into their psychic structures and represent them in dream and fantasy images (Volkan, Ast and Greer, 2002).

Giving the shirt off one's back, as the English saying goes, means trying to please or submit to someone. During previous occasions, Hamilton had referred to his father as Hitler when he remembered times the older man beat him in the "torture chamber." In the dream I stood for Hitler/father. He recalled that when he was a child, his mother had a blue dress with a checkered design. By wearing a shirt with the same color and design, Hamilton was feminizing himself and submitting himself as a woman to his brutal father. By putting himself into a homosexual position, he was making an attempt to avoid punishment by his father/me. In a sense, as was typical for him, he was putting the punishment he expected from his father under his own "control" by taking refuge in a homosexual position. Also, I sensed, he thought that if he submitted to me sexually, I might not leave him. But after this session I took my Christmas vacation and we missed three sessions.

FOWLER: Anal themes shift somewhat to homosexual themes as his associations to his dream link you with Nazis, and his father. You understand this as his effort to control you through submitting to you.

VOLKAN: Here Hamilton is beginning to construct dreams with a "foreigner" (foreign analyst) as the central character. It is a sign that he is now experiencing me as more central. So I am there to meet him. In fact, this is a powerful development because there are no props between him and me. For Hamilton, I am Hitler. He wants to placate me in order to control me, and stop me from hurting him. Just now, his real rage is the bubbling up in the "pişmiş" transference .

FOWLER: Your enthusiasm for this development is refreshing. So often young therapists speak in fearful tones about the patient's hateful feelings. The therapist experience such negative affects as a bad sign, as if something is going wrong in the therapy.

VOLKAN: For Hamilton and for many patients, childhood traumas with the associated unconscious fantasies lead to the development of dangerous objects, which can be felt internally or externalized onto real objects outside, such as the analyst—these individuals then expect other people to treat them in traumatizing ways. It is a protective defense to anticipate the repetition, but it is also an unconscious effort to rework the original trauma. So for Hamilton, I am Hitler in this particular story. Hamilton fears that if he doesn't behave in a pleasing way that I will punish him. In his fantasy, he blasts people/and me in the transference. I want his fantasy to emerge in the analysis fully; therefore, I give him subtle hints that he can bring this to me, there is not anxiety on my part. He is not the first analysand who called me "Hitler." A great deal of clinical experience and professional education has given me an ability to tolerate this. Hamilton's calling me "Hitler" does not disturb me. In reality I am pleased that he can bring an aspect of his scary childhood trauma, the mental conflicts, and the fantasies associated with it to analysis now in such an intensive way. Going through analysis at times is very painful and anxiety provoking; but, without seeing what scares him or her, an analysand cannot find solutions.

After the Christmas vacation, Hamilton returned to work with me and informed me that he had kept the pineapple upside-down cake locked in his car's trunk for days. When the cake started to smell, he had to remove it from the trunk and throw it into a garbage bin. In fact, he added, he had to wash the trunk of his car in order to get rid of the smell. He then calmly reported on some business ventures and told me how he clearly understood how he made "inky messes" in some of his business affairs too. He said that he was tired of spending so much time cleaning up his "inky messes" at his lawyer's office or bank buildings. He seemed to be avoiding the intensity of the therapeutic play that had developed between us just before the Christmas vacation. He was talking emotionally about his business associates, lawyers and bankers, but not directly about me or his feelings about getting rid of the smelly cake, and washing his car's trunk (a symbolic enema). So, I decided not to inquire about his business ventures. I just listened to him and waited for the transference to heat up again.

In a few days' time, he moved to a new house in Richmond and put a new carpet on the stairways going to "the second floor." The carpet had three colors: red, white and blue, the colors of the American flag! He was turning himself into a nice boy wrapped in the American flag. I thought he was telling me that no Turk or Nazi in his or her right mind would punish him! But, by "accident," one day he dropped some fluids on his new carpet and made a stain, an "inky mess."

He spent a great deal of time removing the stain while he turned himself into a Nazi. He imagined putting a turkey (my image) into an oven and cooking it, or he imagined putting me into a gas chamber. Sitting behind him and seeing his rage emerge so clearly, I was delighted with the heating up of his transference relationship to me, but I kept my feelings to myself. However, he sensed my feeling of pleasure, most likely by the way I said "Hm! Hm!" This pleased him and also scared him. However, he said that if he were able to speak about his infantile rage freely, this was an improvement. But, he still expected me to function, not as a "new" person, but like people of his childhood. I could still be someone who might punish him. I waited and noticed that Hamilton took a chance to "experiment" further, expressing his rage openly. This time he was "free" in his dreams "to shit" everywhere. In a few dreams, he saw himself as a three or four-year-old boy wearing short pants and going from room to room. There were toilets in each room and he used them.

FOWLER: You are delighted in the way the transference relationship is developing even when Hamilton is imagining you as a Nazi, or reversing the roles by transforming you into a Christmas turkey and placing you in a gas chamber. I think you model for students, and for relatively junior therapists, the ease with which you can accept the transference as a crucial part of Hamilton's emotional growth and psychic development.

VOLKAN: This is part of the play so essential to Hamilton's experiencing his affects as tolerable and safe. You see, he is deeply puzzled by his parents punishing him. We might imagine young Hamilton saying, "What did I do that was so bad?" In chaotic homes where parents act out physical punishment without clear explanation of the cause, the children will create their own explanations. Hamilton is now replaying the stories with me, inserting me into the storyline. This is precisely where he needs to go. As an analyst, you have to be confident that this kind of negative imagery is part of his conscious and unconscious work. You don't want to shy away from the negative and only join when the patient senses you as a good object. I see this failure in supervision quite frequently. A therapist calls me and says, "What am I going to do with the anger of this patient?" I say, "My God, this is a patient!" I tell the therapist to relax and listen to the story that is unfolding. I try and help the therapist understand why they are so averse to the anger of a patient. There are times when supervision is about teaching the therapist how to stay with the patient in such moments.

FOWLER: That's the attitude that is so important to communicate. Hamilton comes with such trauma and he is filled with rage. If he is to mend the splits and tolerate his affects, he must have a new experience with you, so you invite his internal world onto the stage of the analysis. You delight in it.

Throughout this period in his analysis—still the third year of our working together—he remained with Michelle and dated no one else. Michelle, herself, had a nice home not too far away from Hamilton's new home. Michelle had a daughter in her early teens. Hamilton liked Michelle's daughter, but had no close relationship with her. When he wined and dined Michelle, they would not take her daughter with them, and for sex they would use Hamilton's place. One day while visiting Michelle's house, Hamilton suddenly noticed how angry Michelle's daughter was with her mother. The next day on my couch when he reported this, he felt very anxious. He wondered if the teenager felt angry because of feelings of rejection by her mother who was spending a great deal of time with Hamilton. Michelle's daughter reminded him of himself as a rejected child. What was "hot," however, was Hamilton's experiencing the teenager as a sibling competing for Michelle's (mother's/Abigail's) love. This induced feelings of sibling rivalry and a new wave of discomfort in him. This time, instead of freely verbalizing his rage, he felt sleepy. For all practical purposes, he had given up the symptom of falling asleep on my couch, and now he could not fall asleep, but just felt sleepy. I sensed that he was afraid of punishment and wanted to become an opossum again, so I encouraged him to stay awake and continue to talk to me. In a trance-like state, with accompanying emotions, he re-experienced being on the second floor of the second farm house, in front of the "torture chamber." He said, "I am at the bathroom door. It is not painted. It is made of pine. Stained pine." His experience, I sensed, was vivid. He was noticing the smallest details of the entrance to the "torture chamber." He added, "I am waiting!" and went into a paralyzing silence. After a minute or so, I said, "You are waiting!" With anxiety in his voice, Hamilton began to speak again. "Because my father is beating up my brother . . . My brother is screaming . . . Torture chamber . . . It is going to hurt . . . I don't want to be hurt. There is no escape. Where can I go? I'll be caught! I'll be caught!" I asked him who was going to catch him. He replied, "My mother! We live on a farm . . . No place to go . . . It [his entering into the torture chamber] is inevitable!" He went into the paralyzing silence again while I waited. Hamilton again began to describe what he was experiencing. "I can't see my father beating my brother. The door is closed . . . But I can imagine . . . My father makes him pull down his pants. My father says (Hamilton imitated his father's voice), 'Dance! Dance!' . . . Oh! I fear my father's anger." Then Hamilton described to me how angry his father and mother were when they whipped him. He imitated his father's voice again. "It is for your own good. It hurts me more than it hurts you!" Then Hamilton stopped mimicking his father's voice and said, "I don't believe them. I want to say something to them. I want to say something to them." I replied, "You are safe here. Feel free to say what you wanted to tell them." Hamilton then addressed his parents about his childhood and screamed, "I want to punish you! I want to hurt you!"

He went back to recalling his brother in the "torture chamber." He said, "My brother goes into the bathroom first . . . My brother is sobbing, crying! My mother told my father to whip us. I don't know what we had done."

I was aware that he had not yet put himself in the bathroom. He was still outside and waiting. I thought that this was a "hot" time for him to recall more, so I said to him, "You are still waiting at the door. What will happen after your brother comes out?" Hamilton went back to imitating his father's voice. "Come in! You misbehaved!" and then went into a long silence. I stayed silent, too, and he resumed talking with his father's voice. "You did not pick up your clothes. I don't want to punish you. You have to do what I tell you. You have to obey your mother. If I don't punish you, you will not grow up to be a good boy. Are you sorry? Are you sorry?" Now Hamilton began to speak with his own voice. "I am sorry. I am sorry. I'll not do it again. Please don't whip me . . . I plead for your mercy" . . . After another tense silence, Hamilton whispered, "I feel so powerless . . . shattered . . . It is so humiliating!" I said, "Hm! Hm!" in a way that showed my empathy for him. The session came to an end and he left.

FOWLER: Hamilton experiences another therapeutic regression in these sessions in which he experienced the vivid memories of standing in front of the bathroom (torture chamber) door. The memory and experience is evocative and terrifying.

VOLKAN: Hamilton is going through an emotional reaction to his memories. Now in the session with me he is going to tolerate his affects and have a new experience—one that he can put into words, rather than live out through paranoid fears of dark empty parking garages.

FOWLER: You do not try to sooth him or talk him out of it, you invite him to go deeper, you say, "You are safe here, feel free to say whatever you want to them." He tells them he wants to punish them and hurt them. This appears to be a crucial moment in the treatment. Can you describe the importance of this therapeutic moment to Hamilton's internal development?

VOLKAN: Let me start from the concept, "therapeutic regression." When Hamilton comes seeking analysis he is in a regressed state, compulsively living out the need for an "angel" every night, then moving on before the woman rejects him. He is compulsively seeking a solution to the experience of having Abigail as his love object, then losing her, having a good mother, and being rejected by her. Finding a woman every night is a symptom, just as not being able to sleep with the same women on any consecutive night is a symptom. What psychoanalysis does by inviting the patient to lie on the couch, facing away from the analyst, is to take away certain realities pertaining to the analyst. By taking away some pressures of social discourse (including attending to analyst's facial expressions and subtle nonverbal communications) this induces more fantasies on the part of the analysand about the analyst. So Hamilton begins his analysis using defenses to block out the traumas, then he regresses (with the help of the analytic setting) in order to visit the traumas and conflicts that trouble him. In the analysis Hamilton uses what psychological resources he has in order to relive realistic, fantasized childhood associated with mental conflicts, unconscious fantasies, symptom, and personality organization formations in the transference—this is the action of the analysis. When that process is finished, Hamilton will creatively alter the effects of the traumas and discover more mature and adaptive defenses—he will experiment. When he becomes more secure in his new defenses, he will again return to the conflict in order to work through the conflicts. That is the progression. Each time he returns to the conflict Hamilton will alter the story and its outcome with new feelings and understanding. And I will go there with him, observing the dangers and fantasies, translating them into usable adult language and experience.

So, in this set of sessions Hamilton is using all kinds of things to deal with his memories of the torture chamber—now he goes back to face it. It is the end result of his therapeutic regression. After this, he will review the habitual ways he dealt with these traumas, and in the process he will go back to his old ways a little bit, which is frustrating to him at that time. The new ways of facing his scary internal objects is not yet established; but the old ways are not good enough any more. So, Hamilton will move back-and-forth as he experiments with new adaptations and ways of relating until he feels more secure and more mature. This will take some time and is what we call working through. He will go back to some anal patterns again, but not as hot as this one. This mental approach to the door of the torture chamber is critical to his facing his scary internal father, but he stops at the door. I want him to go in, symbolically, to face his internal scary father. This therapeutic story and therapeutic regression is pişmiş. This is the visit that really starts his healing and development! Now he will try new things.

During the next session he reported a fantasy of taking Dorothy's pants off and touching her vagina. I told him that he had sexualized his powerlessness and humiliation and wanted to do to his sister what his father had done to him. This time he said "Hm! Hm!" indicating his agreement with me.

By our next session he reported noticing a big change in himself and explained this change. He admitted that since the beginning of his analysis, whether he reported to me or hid it from me, he always experienced an internal feeling of anger. After the recent experiences on the couch, he began having what he called "normal" feelings. This was so unusual for him, a big change. After our last session, he only had "normal" feelings. He then described what he meant by "normal" feelings. "Yesterday, while driving on Monument Avenue (in Richmond), I noticed new spring flowers in gardens." He said, "The flowers were nice and beautiful; they gave me pleasure."

After experiencing "normal" feelings, Hamilton stopped seeing Michelle's daughter as a sibling and Michelle, herself, as an idealized mother who loved only Hamilton or at least loved Hamilton more than anyone else. At this time, he and Michelle had been dating for nine months. One day Hamilton told me he was aware that he had been using Michelle as a "sacrificial lamb." He explained what he meant by this term. He needed a woman with whom he could practice going to bed on consecutive nights and also practice exclusive dating. He felt that now he had enough practice and he could go on to deal with his other problems. Interestingly enough, Hamilton said he had become fond of Michelle and her daughter. But, at this point in his life, he was not yet ready to commit himself to a marriage or even to a long-term relationship. He, I sensed, also experienced some remorse for using Michelle as a "sacrificial lamb" as well as hurting her daughter. He decided to talk with Michelle about their sexual relationship.

They mutually agreed to cease being lovers. Michelle and Hamilton would remain friends.

Chapter 5
Madonna and the Dead Child

After undergoing psychoanalysis for almost three-and-a-half years, Hamilton was acting like a carefree and secure little boy exploring nature. He dated other women after separating from Michelle, but his urgent need to sleep with a woman every night was gone. Furthermore, he was no longer "paranoid" while walking in empty, semi-dark parking lots. He noticed different kinds of spring flowers in the gardens of his neighborhood, as well as other beautiful things in his surroundings. He reported admiring a painting he saw while visiting an office of another industrialist. On the couch he was animated.

One day he told me that the night before he had discovered a key to truly comprehending something I had told him many months earlier. It involved my telling him how he seemed to divide himself and the people around him into "black" and "white" categories. Although he was aware that he was dividing himself and his companions, he could not emotionally comprehend my telling him that it was difficult for him to make "gray" by blending "black" and "white." One moment a woman was an "angel," and the next moment she was a "witch." How could the same person be a loved "angel" and a hated "witch" at the same time? The night before this discussion took place between us, he was watching a film on television about a Mafia boss and his men. Watching one particular scene, Hamilton suddenly realized how "love" and "hate" meet at one point. He described how one of the men in the film was the favorite of the Mafia boss. When this man broke the Mafia rules, however, the boss fed him lavishly, kissed him on the lips, and then killed him unceremoniously: The kissing and the killing merged, in a sense, into one point in time.

Hamilton spoke of how the idea of "love" and "hate" coming together and touching one another was a new emotional experience for him. Intellectually, he knew that a woman he wished to punish—or even murder—in his fantasy was the same woman he idealized the day or the month before; but still he could not comprehend that she was "loved" and "hated" at the same time. In other words, until then Hamilton did not "know," nor could he fully experience what it is like to love and hate someone simultaneously, since experiencing "grayness" was not part of his psychic repertoire. I told him that "loving and hating" simultaneously is called *ambivalence.* I explained to Hamilton that when a person experiences ambivalence, he or she mends the image of the other person who is simultaneously loved and hated and, in turn, one mends his or her own self.

FOWLER: After Hamilton's growth-promoting regression, he begins to experience "normal" emotions and then experiences a remarkable development—He begins to comprehend how love and hate can be felt for the same person at the same time. He talks about love and hate and how he can now see them together. How did this happen?

VOLKAN: He did this by sleeping with Michelle two nights in a row. It should be recalled that in the past the "good" woman would become the "bad" woman the next night. Hamilton faced this anxiety every night he stayed with her. This is what he referred to as "experimenting." By putting the idealized "angel" side by side with the "devil" of a woman he faced the anxiety in action, but at first he was not consciously aware of doing this. When he experienced Michelle as "bad" she did not torture him. Hamilton emotionally realizes, "My god! I am putting opposites together. I am taming the aggression in dangerous women and me. This is what I do!" From that time on I know that he will be capable to think and feel like a neurotic person. Before he never tested the possibility that Michelle was a full person, with good and bad qualities—he had to discover this! When I start working with patients who utilize defensive splitting excessively, I notice that in spite of the fact intellectually they know that the intimate other is one person, experientially they do not know that a person can love and hate the other while this person remains as the same person.

Three years and six months after Hamilton's analysis began, he became involved in a therapeutic play of further mending images—his own and others'. I was absent from my office for a period of ten days because of an overseas trip, and I resumed working with Hamilton on my return, only to leave him again two weeks later for another overseas trip that lasted three weeks. Hamilton was not given any reason for my absences, but he was told beforehand that I would not be available to him on these two separate occasions. Analysands always respond emotionally to their analysts' absences. Analysands are in regressed states due to their neuroses and/or due to their "therapeutic regressions" that allow them to "re-experience" their real, as well as fantasized childhood desires, fears and expectations of people in their environment. When a person is in a regressed state, separation from an important person—the analyst—makes an impact on that person.

Before I took my first overseas trip, I knew that my double absences would take place at an unfortunate time for Hamilton. At this time he was very actively and emotionally involved in understanding why he had been "splitting" his and his companions' mental images into "good" and "bad" categories, treating them as if they were two separate individuals at different times. He was also making serious initial attempts to mend his own self, as well as his mental perceptions of others. Luckily, and because of Hamilton's inner determination to get well, my two absences further stimulated Hamilton's "mending" activities. They also allowed him to bring to his consciousness the deepest reason why the "two absences" of his mother, after delivering Hamilton's two younger siblings, had been psychologically devastating for him as a child, and why it had initiated in him an unconscious fantasy to be his mother's only baby and "kill" his siblings, especially the two younger sisters.

FOWLER: The two absences in the analysis serve as a parallel for Hamilton's early childhood experiences of maternal absence. But for an analysand in a therapeutic regression, would any approximation of absence serve as a similar catalyst? In other words, was it necessary for Hamilton to experience two separations in order to stimulate this process?

VOLKAN: I did not deliberately want him to have a hard time or remember and work through his mother's "absences" after delivering Hamilton's two younger sisters. This brings us to the discussion of what is called "Corrective Emotional Experience." When I was younger, Franz Alexander and Thomas French's (1946) therapeutic concept of a therapist deliberately attempting to be a better object than a patient's childhood objects was much discussed. Alexander and French thought that this would be helpful in altering the patient's bad experiences from his or her childhood. Their concept was generally rejected by the psychoanalytic establishment because it creates the illusion that the analyst is all knowing authority capable of forcing change in the internal world of the patient. Returning to Hamilton's treatment, I did not deliberately attempt to be a better mother or father to him by designing actions on my part. If my two absences did not take place he would find other external stimuli or an internal ones, like a dream, to remember, and work through the psychological meaning of his mother's two pregnancies in his actions outside of the analytic sessions, but most importantly in a "pişmiş" transference too.

Before I left on my first trip, Hamilton fantasized that I was taking my two "vacations" in order to have sexual affairs with different women. In reality, my two overseas trips were in relation to my involvement in "unofficial diplomacy" and my attempts to study the psychology of international relationships. Ten years prior to my meeting Hamilton, I was a member of the American Psychiatric Association's (APA) Committee on Foreign Affairs. This committee became involved in bringing influential Israeli and Egyptian (and later Palestinian) delegates together every four or five months for a series of "unofficial" diplomatic dialogues. This series of meetings lasted for six years until 1986. The next year I created the Center for the Study of Mind and Human Interaction (CSMHI) at the University of Virginia. The faculty of this Center included—besides psychoanalysts, psychiatrists and psychologists—former U.S. diplomats and well-known historians.

VOLKAN: For information about the Center for the Study of Mind and Human Interaction (CSMHI) and its activities see: Vamık D. Volkan, The Need to Have Enemies and Allies: From Clinical Practice to International Relationships; Bloodlines: From Ethnic Pride to Ethnic Terrorism, Blind Trust: Large Groups and their Leaders in Times of Crisis and Terror and Killing in the Name of Identity: Stories of Bloody Conflicts. *The Center was closed in 2004 after my retirement from the University of Virginia and becoming a Professor Emeritus.*

In fact, many veterans of the Israeli-Arab dialogue series constituted the core faculty of my new Center. While none of them had offices in the house at the Blue Ridge Hospital where Hamilton came for his analysis, I also used this house as the headquarters to administrate CSMHI. After Hamilton started working with me, I received a grant for ethno-political work and I found myself investing more and more time and energy in my new "career." My two trips were funded by this grant. I felt guilty (but not overwhelmingly so) about my upcoming absences from my analysands, including Hamilton, of course. A thought came to my mind: my new "career" was like having a new "baby."

FOWLER: Your analytic attitude is clear even when he is not in the analytic session. You begin musing about your new career—you play with the idea that the career is a new baby that takes you away from Hamilton. It is interesting how in tune you are with his story.

VOLKAN: In tune, but only in my fantasy—these thoughts fall under the umbrella of counter-transference, or better a counter response, in the service of maintaining the story. I do not share these musings with Hamilton. This would place an unwanted burden on his mind. But in my mind it fits with the birth of his sisters and the reaction Hamilton had to these births.

FOWLER: In recent years some psychoanalysts have recommended disclosing such fantasies—what Owen Renik (1999) calls "Laying your cards on the table."

VOLKAN: Starting with Freud, we have developed a workable frame for conducting analysis, and this frame provides a space for the freedom of the patient to play in the security of this space. The analyst plays with the patient's productions, but should not use the analysis to gratify the wish to explore his or her mind. If Hamilton opens up the story of the birth of his sisters, if I feel that my countertransference response helps us to collect more proof that we are dealing with a hot issue and if there is an appropriate time to further increase the therapeutic alliance I might tell Hamilton what had come to my mind. In reality I did not tell Hamilton that my new career was like my having a new baby. The idea of "laying your cards on the table" gives the younger therapist a wrong message. I recall a case that was presented to me some years ago at a psychoanalytic institute. The analysand sees a cockroach on the floor and while lying on the couch he points out the bug to his female analyst. The analyst has fears about cockroaches (I do not know the reasons). So she asks the patient to help her to get rid of the cockroach, which by that time has disappeared under the couch. Both the patient and the analyst get up from their locations and kneel down on the floor and search for the cockroach together. They do not find it. After this "togetherness" on the floor the patient goes to the couch and the analyst takes her place behind the couch and also tells the patient more about her fears of cockroaches. This event was presented as an example of how in a "modern" version of psychoanalysis sharing things with the patient is so wonderful! To hear this case report and the conclusion of the usefulness of the event scared me. It takes a great deal of work, study, proper personal analysis, long supervisions in order to become an analyst. To perceive its caricature as the real thing in the so-called pluralistic and democratic atmosphere of psychoanalysis of today in the USA saddens me.

I was going to leave Hamilton like his mother had left him when she had two new babies. I did not share my thoughts with Hamilton before I left for my first trip, but I wanted to hear from him how he would react to this separation between us. Instead, I spoke with him about his fantasy of my going away to find women and have sexual affairs with them. I told him that during our past separations, it was he who sought women, including a Turkish woman, in an attempt to deal with his feelings about losing me. This time, I told him, he was projecting his own image onto me, imagining me as the one who seeks and finds women when the two of us are separated. I explained further that his fantasy meant that he was trying to deny the separation between us, since wherever I went I would be carrying him (the image of him which he projected onto me) within me. I added that his identifying me with him or he with me could also be useful as he developed new psychological functions that deal with separations in ways that did not repeat old patterns of response. Through our previous work together, I said, he had learned a great deal about the meaning of separations from important others. By identifying with the experiences he has with me, he might observe impulses that arise due to my upcoming absences and wonder about them. Finally, I told him that I would be interested to hear about his observations. We parted and I took my first overseas trip.

On Monday, after returning from my first trip, Hamilton said, "Welcome back!" as soon as he took his place on my couch. I responded to him by stating that I was ready to resume our work together. He remarked that he had no idea where I had been, but supposed I had attended some professional meeting. This time he was speculating on a more realistic explanation for my absence. He was glad to have me back. He said that during the ten days of my absence he had felt relatively contented and had not gotten into "any mischief." He joked about not having published any advertisements for women. He had not searched for new women.

Although he seemed to be in a relaxed mood when I saw him on Monday, he left his trench coat on during our session and this puzzled me. It was a cool spring day and, although he had come in wearing a trench coat, ordinarily he would have taken his coat off before lying down. My room was warm, and on my couch, clad in a trench coat, he looked like a caricature of a spy from the pages of MAD magazine. My first thought was that he wanted to spy on me to discover what I had done while I was away. He was certainly curious about my activities during my absence, but I did not tell him about them, waiting instead to see what would develop. As I watched him, I sensed that his wearing the trench coat while lying on my couch had a second meaning. He was using his coat to protect his body and his turned-up collar to protect his neck. I recalled how in the past he had thought of me as "a Terrible Turk," capable of beheading him with a scimitar. I concluded that, despite his pleasure at seeing me, and in spite of his telling me how well he had been during my absence, he was afraid of me. I decided to see what would develop and therefore did not say much during this session.

The reader will recall that I did not see Hamilton on Tuesdays. When he returned on Wednesday, Hamilton lay on the couch without his trench coat. He informed me that he heard, during my absence, that his first cousin's daughter was leaving her husband. The woman was in her late thirties, and she lived some distance away. Since his separation from Michelle, Hamilton had been dating a few "regulars" and could now tolerate being without a woman some nights. The news about his cousin's daughter led him to consider dating her. Then he heard my voice within him saying, "You should not do this." I had never given him such an order, so it was clear that he had created a mental image of me within himself prohibiting his involvement with his cousin's daughter. He had not identified with my image, but kept it as an unassimilated "foreign body" in his mind that would talk to him and give him an order. If he truly identified with me, he would not experience me as someone separate, even I was located within him. If the identification had taken place, it would be him talking to himself. Hamilton did not call the woman, even after acquiring her telephone number. He considered this restraint a sign of success, and was pleased with himself, although I knew that he still had a long way to go. It was not he who prohibited involvement in an incestuous-like activity, but rather it was my unassimilated "voice" which ordered him not to do so.

When Hamilton wondered why he had not told me about his cousin's daughter on the first day we resumed our work, I reminded him that he was wearing his trench coat on the couch that day. I told him that on Monday he saw me not only as a censor, but also as someone who might punish him for exhibiting a derivative of his old incestuous impulses. He agreed and displayed insight by remarking that the return of his incestuous impulses and/or "need" to find a new woman was a response to our separation. Hamilton recalled that once I had told him that he would control his impulses when his "needs" became his "wishes." He did not need to have his cousin's daughter; he only wished to have her.

Hamilton continued to talk, and he was curious about an event that had taken place the day before. He said that, contrary to his success in controlling his impulse to date his first cousin's daughter, he had done something "stupid" and given in to another impulse between our Monday and Wednesday sessions.

On Tuesday, an acquaintance named Harold came to Hamilton's office to discuss a small motel that was for sale. Assuming that the motel in question was worth about six hundred and fifty thousand, Hamilton impulsively offered six hundred thousand and bought it on the spot. In his fantasy, he would quickly make a profit of fifty thousand on the resale of the motel. But, a visit to his purchased building on Tuesday afternoon brought Hamilton back to reality. The truth was that it would fetch no more than five hundred and fifty thousand, so his impulsive buying had cost him at least fifty thousand. Listening to his story, I sensed that he symbolically "castrated" himself for his incestuous desire; he was not wearing his trench coat collar up on Tuesday!

Hamilton was irritated with himself because he had been able to say "no" to one impulse but not to another. Just as he idealized his women, he had idealized the motel in his fantasy and convinced himself that he needed to have it immediately, without considering whether or not it would be good for him. In this case, his idealized building cost him money. He said he wished he could tame his responses to tempting offers that he knew should realistically be evaluated first. He ended the session by recalling once more how I had told him in the past that I perceived he had a problem making gray—that it could be achieved by blending black and white, and by putting a border around his impulses. He added that it was now time to mend his perception of his women and himself once and for all. I said, "Let's see what will evolve."

Hamilton's reference for gray and making borders appeared in his Wednesday night dream, which he reported on Thursday:

> I dreamed of the farm where I grew up and spent my childhood. A piece of land on the farm was being cleared by bulldozers to create a preserve where nature could take its course, new vegetation could grow, and animals would be encouraged to live. Workmen were nailing down brass signs designating the borders of this cleared land: they bore the logo of the University of Virginia. The soil was gray, although in reality that region of Virginia has red soil.

Hamilton reported a second dream immediately after the first. In this one, Abigail's brother Morris, appearing as a teenager, seized Hamilton by the hands and ordered him to get down on his knees. In college Hamilton had been on a wrestling team, and at one point he had a match with an opponent whose hands were uncommonly strong. The dream brought this to mind. In the dream Hamilton was forced to his knees, whereby Morris asked him to perform fellatio. Recognizing this as a homosexual act, Hamilton tried different wrestling maneuvers to avoid it, but could not overpower Morris.

After reporting both dreams, Hamilton spontaneously began to assign associations to them. By now, due to our work on his past dreams, Hamilton sensed that some observations or events during the daytime might stimulate the dream(s) of the following night. In psychoanalysis, we call such observations or events "day residues." Hamilton did not know this technical term, but his associations were related to what, in reality, might be the starting points of his dreams. He said that when he had moved to his new house, he did not like the color of his bedroom walls. They were painted a rose color, and in his mind this color was "feminine." He had spoken of repainting his bedroom walls, and apparently, during my ten days' absence, he sent two persons from one of his factories to his home and told them to paint the walls light yellow. On Wednesday, before he had the two dreams, he noticed that the bedroom walls did not look yellow as they were supposed to, but were gray instead, since yellow paint had been applied over the existing rose that he had disliked for some time, but had not bothered to change until I went away. When he noticed the gray color of his bedroom walls, he recalled my equating making gray with a capacity for psychic integration. He then recalled a dream that he had a year earlier. In this dream he was in college and a member of the wrestling team, but he was wearing pink trunks that made him look effeminate. Before going to sleep, it had occurred to him that making gray would represent not only an attempt at integration, but also an effort to be manly—changing rose pink to gray. Before he had his two dreams on Wednesday night, Hamilton acknowledged to himself that his being a "woman addict" had something to do with his problems concerning his manliness. He defensively needed to prove to himself that he was a "man" by arranging unending sexual activities.

Associating to his first dream reported on Thursday, he thought that the piece of land where new life was to be celebrated represented his wished-for integrated self. The University of Virginia logo represented me, inasmuch as I was a professor at the University of Virginia, who was conducting his analysis at the Blue Ridge Hospital grounds that belonged to the University of Virginia. The logo Hamilton dreamed about is the letter "V" (which stands, also in the actual logo, for "Virginia") with two swords crossing one another under the letter "V." Hamilton understood that "V" also stood for "Volkan" and two swords clashing made me a phallic father set against a (Oedipal) son.

The brass markers evoked another association for Hamilton—a dream reported six months earlier. In this dream he had seen a Roman flag holder made of brass and broken in two. At the time we were investigating his "need" to possess many women. Since "brass" brought "big brass" (persons of importance) to mind, this mainly represented his idealized, narcissistic self. The top of the flag holder had many snake-like protrusions (symbolic penises) that represented his fear of castration (broken flag holder) and of not being as big as his brother or father. If he had many penises (and, correspondingly, many women), he could defend himself against his worries about castration.

In the current Wednesday night dream I was the big brass; he had projected his childhood vision of omnipotence onto the image of the father/analyst. The dream represented his making me a strong Oedipal father. I was clearing part of his psychic space, making room for an integrated (gray) locus for a new life (ego and superego). He commented with insight that his analysis (his taking my image into him) had enabled him to say "no" to his impulse toward his cousin's daughter.

Hamilton provided some further details of his first dream, saying that the gray color of the soil was not soothing but that it reminded him of the color of Nazi uniforms. I suggested he might perceive his wish to take me in (identification with me) to show him how to make gray and set limits (borders) as alarming, because of his childhood experience with his father. I noted that he wanted to identify with his father, who had, in fact, beaten and humiliated him. I made reference to his perception of me entering him (as symbolized by the University logo entering his newly developing psychic arena), and Morris's semen entering him. Morris was assigned to clean little Hamilton's bottom. While adult Hamilton had no memory of Morris doing anything inappropriate to him, he thought that Abigail's brother might sexually stimulate him.

FOWLER: In this dream, Hamilton associates to the symbol of the grey soil. This is a great example of splitting transforming to ambivalence. But there seem to be many dangers including homosexual fears.

VOLKAN: Yes, Hamilton is returning now to the development of ambivalence. He has discovered ambivalence, but he is not yet fully able to maintain it. Hamilton will continue at least for a while to experience the old fears associated with the splitting of objects into all good and all bad. While he is experimenting with ambivalent relationship, at this point his symbol of grey soil is infused with aggressive affects and is therefore dangerous.

Hamilton had to take a strong and caring man into himself in order to gain strength, but at the same time he dreaded submission (as indicated by the homosexual posture). I said that his father had symbolically and aggressively "raped" him and that, although he had been a helpless child at the time, he felt aggression toward his father and now toward me as well, perceiving me as terrifying. He needed me to be strong and caring to be a model for identification. But still he could not make me gray except in terms of Nazi gray, and he did not yet find the gray soil soothing. We needed to further understand the aggression that was present in our interaction and to further differentiate his wished-for image of a strong and caring man from the "rapist" image of his original father. He seemed able to hear this and to understand it.

It should be recalled that, although he is not Jewish, Hamilton used the image of Hitler and Nazi Germany to refer to his own childhood environment, especially his visits to the "torture chamber." He now told me that he was reading a book on Hitler in order to once more master his childhood fear of his father. I told Hamilton that in his mind my image as an analyst was still intertwining, or at least competing, with his Hitler/father image. I said that as long as he modeled me after Hitler, like a punitive father, it would be hard for him to take me in and retain the insights brought forth in our work together.

On Friday Hamilton continued associating in his dreams, further exploring his wish and attempts to mend his own image and those of intimate others' (father's and mother's). He told me that something else in his house was still rose-colored (feminine): one of the toilets. On Wednesday, before having his two dreams, he checked this toilet and noticed that it was cracked. He was determined that the crack (split) be repaired. Then a rather unusual, if not bizarre, thought occurred to him that a dentist, who mends cracks in people's teeth, would surely know how to mend cracks in any kind of enamel or ceramic surface. At the time, he thought of a dentist as a "mender." He impulsively called an older Richmond dentist whom he knew, and at first the man laughed at Hamilton's bizarre request. But on Thursday he came to Hamilton's house and mended the crack with some adhesive. Hamilton was overwhelmed by the dentist's kindness and described this event to me on Friday. He and I were able to discuss how he had turned to a man (a father image) to help him to mend the crack. As a dentist this man represented a frightening, drilling, castrating, attacking father, but then he turned out to be a caring, repairing, mending father. Hamilton was making gray by merging a frightening dentist (or analyst) with a kind dentist (or analyst). We discussed how, as his father/analyst image became better integrated and less laden with aggression, the gray would become more soothing. In turn, he could identify with such an analyst and further mend his own and his women's previously split images.

We had one more week before my second absence, an absence that would be rather long, three weeks. On the second Monday of the two-week period before I left again, he began the session by reporting a new dream in which he saw his childhood home. The attic looked larger in the dream than it had really been, and he knew that this dream referred to his efforts to change his inner psychic structure. Old family letters and photographs were stored in the attic, and when he was little his mother had asked him periodically to take this or that box filled with family mementoes up there. The attic stood for a psychic container in which he kept stories of his family, both good and bad. Hamilton's parents came from "good backgrounds," but his family was not without its "secrets"—sordid things like whippings, enemas, the need to make perfect stools, and depression. Hamilton recalled taking his sister Dorothy to the attic when both were much younger. He undressed her there and examined her naked body. His family secrets included "incest."

In the dream Hamilton worried lest the ceiling of the attic might be weak, although he thought of the house as solid. He surmised that by dreaming about the attic he was still integrating "good" and "bad" things about his family and his own mind. Much more work was to be done. But, he was happy to note that the house itself (himself) was solid and that the confusion in the attic (his head) would remain tolerable until his internal turmoil settled down and he finished the mending activities.

Second Wednesday (no Tuesday session): Hamilton reported that my upcoming separation might take me to Turkey, and he wondered if, upon my return, I would be the same. He spoke of my "two sides." Although I was always dignified and nice to him, he said, he had an image of me also as a barbarous Turk with a scimitar. He said that he was aware that, when first on my couch, he had occasionally put his hand behind his neck to keep me from beheading him. I suggested that he might be afraid that a trip to Turkey would contaminate me with aggression so that on my return I would beat or cut him up. Laughing nervously, he said, "I am trying to integrate you, too!" He recalled that one of his business associates had spoken of a giant open market in Turkey, saying, "They have all kinds of things there. You'll like that place." I explained to Hamilton that his identification with me was not an "all or none" business. He could choose what he wanted to have from the open market.

The next day, the second Thursday of the two-week period between my absences, he reported that he felt more capable of holding onto what he was learning in his analysis. On the previous night he had visited his older son's house and had thoroughly enjoyed his grandchildren, who seemed healthy and happy. It occurred to him that he had done better than his parents in rearing his older son; he had never beaten him. In turn, his sons were doing better than he in rearing his grandchildren, of whom he felt very proud. Then he reported a dream that involved Harold, the seller of the motel for which Hamilton had paid six hundred thousand, only to realize later that this impulsive purchase had lost him fifty thousand:

> I was going to a large field. A woman was with me as I drove there in a car. In order to get there we had to drive through an open market. It was in a Jamaican village populated by blacks. They were selling various things, including bananas. Harold was on a horse in a Western type saddle. His foot was caught in the saddle, and I told him, "You don't know how to ride a horse; get off and let me get on it." The scene changed; I was in the land I had set out for. I knew that this time it was a place called Deer Fork in Virginia, a place that I knew since my childhood. On this land stood a house I thought of as skimpy.

Hamilton thought that the dream had something to do with his attending a social event that night to raise money for a charity. As he entered the building where this event took place, he noticed an African-American woman at the entrance, collecting invitations at a stand. He asked her to dance, and then began to wonder what people might think of his dancing with an African-American partner. He wondered why he was so worried. He then recalled having gone to Jamaica with his father and older sister after his first wife's death. They rented a house for a week and employed a black cook with whom Hamilton secretly had danced on one occasion. At the party, he realized at last that his anxiety was due to his displacement of Abigail's image onto his dance partner. He recalled his parents' dismissal of Abigail and their failure to appreciate his attachment to her. Then he thought how during his analysis I "approved" his childhood attachment to Abigail and realized that he had internalized my approval. In other words, he was buying my "approval" from the Turkish open market and making it his own. He said that after he realized this, his anxiety disappeared, and he felt free to continue dancing with this African-American woman.

He returned to making associations regarding his dream. He said that the woman in the dream accompanying him in a car to the big field was me, representing a new mother. The open market in Jamaica was superimposed onto the open market in Turkey, to which his business associates had made reference. The image of the open market run by blacks included images of the new mother/Turkish analyst and the "good" Abigail. Bananas were breasts, he said, since as a child he had called his mother's breasts "nanas."

Hamilton wondered why Harold, who had visited Hamilton's office on the previous day, had appeared in this dream. In the dream Hamilton wanted to ride Harold's horse since he felt that he knew better than Harold how to ride the animal. He added that it was a new nutriment, derived from "good" analyst/Abigail/mother and now more integrated, which enabled him to travel to Deer Fork, thereby saying "no" to the impulses represented by Harold.

In the dream he had left the Jamaican/Turkish open market and come to Deer Fork. Hamilton thought that choosing this location was due to the word "fork." He added that Robert Frost, the poet, just came to his mind. After all, Frost had written a famous poem about a fork in the road where one has to choose. He himself was encountering a pathway divided in two, forming a fork. One may stick to a familiar road, repeating old rituals, or courageously choose the "road less traveled." Hamilton said he had chosen the latter in his dream. It took him to a house that represented his new psychic core: integrated but "skimpy"—not yet well developed (much like the attic in the previous dream). Here his associations continued and he recalled more about his dream. Located behind the skimpy house, was another one belonging to someone who had the job of watching over the skimpy house to protect its contents. I reminded him that I was sitting behind him.

Our last session before I left for three weeks, on the second Friday of the two-week period between my absences, was one of the most memorable in Hamilton's analysis. During that hour we came to understand why, during his childhood, his mother had been sunk in the depression that was so largely responsible for his being defensively fixated on splitting the images of intimate others as well as corresponding images of himself. This session opened with the following report of a dream Hamilton called "peculiar":

> It consisted of two words: *Numbers* and *Preservation.*
> Then I saw numbers from one to six. But one of the numbers was missing. It was number three. It was left out. Three was missing.

The day residue of this dream came from a dinner party Hamilton attended that was given by one of his women friends. They had known one another for years and had been lovers from time to time. After separating from Michelle, Hamilton had begun to see this woman, Margaret, without trying either to idealize her or devalue her. By then there was no urgency about having a woman every night, and he was comfortable with Margaret, although sometimes he dated other women.

At Margaret's dinner table, in addition to the hostess, there was a couple and one single man besides Hamilton. There were six chairs set for the five people. Hamilton and the other single man sat at the ends of the rectangular table, and the couple was on one side, with Margaret on the other. One person seemed to be missing. Hamilton first thought that this missing three was the analyst, who was going away for three weeks, but Hamilton sensed that the missing analyst represented something more important. He suddenly realized that until then—three-and-a-half years into his analysis—it had never occurred to him to tell me about a missing sibling.

So I learned for the first time that his parents had six children, the eldest of whom, a girl, died of pneumonia during her first year of life. Only five children survived, and although Hamilton had always spoken of himself as being one of five, he was actually the third survivor among the siblings. The baby's death was referred to in the family as "The Tragedy," and he remembered hearing references to it as a child. He could not remember his dead sister's name at first, but it came to him, along with memories of his mother's depression.

Hamilton now understood that the word preservation concerned preservation of the dead child's, Julia's, memory in his mother's mind. He was sure that his mother had suffered from postpartum depression after the birth of each of her last two daughters, and that her bouts of depression were due to her guilt-ridden, unfinished, complicated mourning over her first baby's death. His mother had certainly been depressed when the family moved to a new location after Abigail's departure: his maternal grandmother had died at about this time also. It seems likely that in Hamilton's mother's mind, the move from the location where Julia was buried and the loss of her mother activated emotions connected with her first child's death. Because of her depression, she was unable to help her son with his own routine development.

When I teach the technique of psychoanalytic treatment to younger colleagues, I always tell them not to "believe" everything in their analysands' initial recollections of personal and family histories. As the transference stories evolve and process, and as repression is lifted, there may be drastic alterations or additions to the histories of what happened long ago. For example, I recall how a young man initially presented the father of his childhood as a tyrant, only to realize in the second year of his analysis how the older man was a kind and loving person. It was the son's childhood fantasies that were responsible for turning his father's image into an image of a tyrant. In Hamilton's case, after three-and-a-half years of analysis, something new and dramatic was added to the history of his developmental years.

As a child, Hamilton heard about Julia's story. He did not repress this knowledge, but "denied" it because of its devastating influence on his psyche. When my two absences were reflected in his mind as his mother's two absences after delivering Hamilton's younger sisters, Hamilton stopped "denying" the story of Julia and their mother's difficulty in grieving for the loss of her first child. Both of us then recalled how Hamilton had made a reference to his mother's unending grief during the first year of his analysis when he displaced the sad situation in his own home with a sad situation in the home of neighbors. When Hamilton was a child, the teenage daughter of a neighboring farm family died. Her parents had a photograph taken of their daughter after her death, and they hung it in their living room where it held a strong fascination for little Hamilton. She looked alive in it. Little Hamilton knew a macabre story concerning this teenager's death. Her parents, not believing that she was gone, needed to be really sure that the person they had buried was their daughter. Furthermore, they wanted to have a last glimpse of her and say farewell. Thus, they had her exhumed six months after her burial. But they were so horrified at the sight of her corpse that they quickly reburied it. Hamilton had been greatly impressed by this bizarre tale, which he mentioned several times. He now realized that he had concealed his family's, especially his mother's, sad story by vividly recalling the neighbor's story.

I would not consider Hamilton a typical "replacement" child—a new child who replaces a dead sibling in his or her mother's mind. But I helped him understand how Julia's death contributed to his defensive creation of an idealized mother/Abigail image that was different from the image of his grieving depressed mother. I suggested that if he understood that his need to search for an idealized woman image in the many women he "collected" was to deny his experience with a depressed mother, this realization would allow him to integrate further female images in general, and in turn his own self-image, thereby testing reality more accurately.

Hamilton stayed silent and appeared sad. He said that he was experiencing his mother's grief and having empathic feelings for her. Suddenly, he became very excited with a new "discovery": He was not the special child in the picture of his mother with a child that was hanging on the wall of his parents' bedroom; the child in the picture was Julia, the one who had died.

FOWLER: Something remarkable has changed after the dream of "Numbers and Preservations." He came to understand that his mother's depression was, at least partly, in reaction to guilt and sadness over Julia's death. He seems to be putting together an image of his mother that is far more complicated than the representation he has carried for fifty years! As he speaks of this Hamilton appears sad, feeling his mother's grief and feeling empathy for her. How do you understand the transformation from only seeing his mother as either all good or all bad to now Hamilton being capable of an more blended and complex representation of his mother?

VOLKAN: He has made mother a more complete human in his mind for whom he can have empathy.

FOWLER: Then he got excited because he realized that he is not the special child in the picture on the wall—the baby in the picture was Julia. How is it that Hamilton has spent his entire adolescent and adult life believing that he was the child in the picture, and how is it possible for him to have such an epiphany in such a condensed fashion? This reworking of his memory, the experience of his mother, and self-image seemed to be related to the series of absences and separations in the analysis. What makes this separation so analyzable, so workable, rather than it being another repetition or trauma for him?

VOLKAN: The answer is what he had done so far in his analytic process. I provided for him a secure environment. He faced the father in the torture chamber. He allowed himself to perceive me as a "Terrible Turk" or Hitler. Nothing bad happened. Both of us survived. A patient who uses defensive splitting is unconsciously and consciously afraid to mend aggressively and libidinally loaded opposite elements. The fantasy is that when you put black and white together the black will overcome the white and you will lose the possibility to hold on to any idealized element. It takes time to own the ability of mending the opposites. He tested mending in various ways. He tested it with Michelle. He has done, in a sense, his own corrective emotional experiences—he initiated them, not I. Now he is ready to test his ability to develop ambivalence and give up defensive splitting for good. He also tested many separations in the transference and observed his reactions to them and understood the reasons for his reactions to separa-

tions. We see him ready to go one more step and stop denying (and partly stop repressing) another painful memory and master the conflict associated with it.

Chapter 6
Shrinking the Torture Chamber

After "mending" his internal world and images of people with whom he related with some degree of intimacy, Hamilton, now in his fourth year on my couch, once more began going over his developmental difficulties and mental conflicts. This time, however, he performed his "review" of childhood from the perspective of a man whose sense of self was different than it had been when he first came to see me. I no longer thought of him as having a personality organization with defensive splitting as the main defense mechanism. He had graduated to a typical "neurotic" personality organization, meaning he now had a cohesive sense of self and could relate to intimate others with ambivalence rather than dividing them into "good" or "bad" categories and experiencing them as if they were two people. I was not surprised that Hamilton began to re-experience his developmental difficulties and mental conflicts once more since, due to my experience with other analysands who had internal worlds similar to Hamilton's, I knew that he now needed to do so for a different reason. This time, when he completed his "review," he would try to get well. He would go beyond mending his sense of self by working on his childhood developmental difficulties and conflicts, especially his Oedipal one. When he began his analysis, he first presented "oral" wishes and fears, "anal" preoccupation, and then some "phallic" and "Oedipal" struggles, primarily in the above order. In the fourth year, after he became a "neurotic" person, he started presenting some primitive forms of "Oedipal" and "phallic" issues first. Then he went back and re-examined his "anal" and "oral" preoccupations and resolved for good his pre-oedipal difficulties and childhood conflicts—before turning to the Oedipal ones again. In this chapter, I will describe his work on Oedipal, phallic and anal-level related conflicts. I will illustrate his re-regression to oral issues in the next chapter. Following this, I will explore his eventual return to more sophisticated Oedipal ones.

His attempt to be involved in an Oedipal triangle (son, mother and father) with a mended self was most primitive, as I observed one day when he appeared to have great discomfort as he lay on my couch. He kept putting his hands behind his neck as if to protect it. I knew that once again I had become a "Terrible Turk" with a scimitar. When he removed his hands from behind his neck he put them into his pockets, checking, I sensed, that his penis was still intact. He was reenacting the University of Virginia logo scenario with its two swords crossing one another, which he had dreamed about previously. But, he was experiencing my "sword" as bigger and stronger, while his "sword" was in danger of being cut off.

He stayed silent, repeatedly moving his hands from the back of his neck to his pockets. He then reported a dream that he called his "three gables" dream. In the dream "three gables"—architectural sections of houses which "stick up"—were standing side by side as if they were squeezed together.

For some weeks prior to the day when he reported this dream, Hamilton had become friendly with a couple in their forties, frequently going to lunch with them. He had heard that this couple was involved in unusual sexual practices. He was fascinated with them. When I heard his dream, instinctively I knew that he was involved in a sexual threesome with this couple. It turned out that his dream was his way of letting me know that this had happened. He was invited to this couple's bed where both men, the woman's husband and Hamilton, took turns having sex with the woman. Hamilton was especially interested in watching the other man's erect penis and his sexual performance.

Hamilton was extremely embarrassed while telling me this story. I waited for a time so that he could experience embarrassment and shame. After awhile, I told him that the title of his dream should be "two gables and one room, or something like that," referring to two penises and one vagina during the sexual threesome (a room is a typical dream symbol for female genitalia). I wondered out loud why he named his dream "three gables." Hamilton then reported that while watching the other man's erected penis he had fantasized about my penis. He had taken my image to the couple's bedroom and compared, in his mind, our sex organs and sexual performances.

The "phallic/Oedipal" incident, however primitive and nearly unsymbolized, was a beginning, opening a new way for Hamilton to re-experience his unresolved Oedipal struggle. In the past, after making love to his stepmother-in-law, he was afraid of being shot by his father-in-law. He experienced paranoid ideation. His father-in-law's image was not internalized in his own self, and therefore would not lead to self-punishment. The danger had remained or projected to outside. His father-in-law's externalized image, for example, lurked in darkness while he was walking in an empty parking lot at dusk. After reporting his "three gables" dream, Hamilton cut off his relationship with the couple; in a sense they were also his "sacrificial lambs" used to bring to life his phallic/Oedipal fantasies. He would never repeat such a threesome. On the couch, at first, he was tortured by feelings of shame and guilt. He acknowledged that he was the owner of incestuous desires. But, more importantly, he now knew that he was also punishing himself by experiencing shame and guilt. He did not need the image of his father-in-law or a burglar to beat him up or shoot him. On my couch he was having a hard time, and I did not come to his rescue. I knew that his owning open feelings of shame and guilt was something new for him, and what he was going through could, in a sense, be considered psychological growing pains.

FOWLER: You do not rescue Hamilton from feelings of shame and guilt. Can you say more about why it is important for him to go through these feelings, and why this is a necessary step?

VOLKAN: Hamilton now has an integrated self, and with this new integrated self he acts out Oedipal impulses in a primitive way. He brings the psychologi-

cal representation of this action into the transference in a dream. He wants to compare his and my/father's penis. But now besides experiencing anxiety and expectation of punishment he also experiences shame and guilt. Shame and guilt give him an emotional insight for owning his Oedipal impulses. When his impulses are owned he can stop his impulses. I am not in the room with him in order to make him feel good all the time. I am in the room with him to help him go through growing pains. At times the analytic work is very painful for the analysand. At other times it provides elation for finding new ego functions that were not previously available for the patient.

As weeks and months passed, he began to experience and report another feeling: remorse. He talked about his past sexual activities involving his sister, sister-in-law, and stepmother-in-law and spoke about how sorry he was for having been involved in such activities. While his sister-in-law and his stepmother-in-law were grown up people when they had sex with him, Hamilton was especially remorseful about what he had done to Dorothy. He and Dorothy had never talked about his night visits to her room and his ejaculating on her legs, and now as an adult, he felt uncomfortable being with her in social settings. Now he could name his feelings associated with his discomfort: shame, guilt, and remorse. He wondered if he should speak with his sister. I gave no advice, and he then told me he was not yet ready to do so.

One day on the couch Hamilton told me that it was therapeutic for him to own and experience such "bad" feelings. After this he felt more comfortable with himself and with me. Soon I noticed a drastic change in his relationship with others, especially with his children. Now he felt like a "father" who loved his children. He reported that his children had noticed the change in him and, in turn, they responded to him with increased closeness. Meanwhile, when he spoke of his grandchildren, he would beam. The fake smile he once pasted on his face was long gone. Instead of being obliged to search for a woman each night, he began to prefer spending many evenings with his older son, his wife, and grandchildren who lived near to him. His daughter and her husband had returned to Northern Virginia and joined an architectural firm in Washington, D.C., and Hamilton now could easily be with her. Driving to Washington about every other month, Hamilton began taking her and her husband to lunch. His younger son was still in another state, and Hamilton began to visit him regularly instead of flying to far away places in order to find a Turkish woman or other idealized "nanas." His "woman addiction" gone, Hamilton began to enjoy reading books during his free time, particularly books on World War II that he read before falling asleep at night. He joked that some stories about World War II were also personalized and stood for his own childhood "wars" with people in his environment and his past preoccupation with me as Hitler.

Hamilton was fascinated with a story about German submarines during World War II. He told me how he learned that the United States Navy had a "blind spot" concerning the enemy submarines, which could cause great damage and destruction. He dreamt of big and mighty enemy submarines. I told him that they might represent other men's/analyst's penises. I also told him that it was better to symbolize such penises and dream about them than observe another man's "unsymbolized" erect penis. He laughed. Hamilton continued to read about World War II, but now, instead of submarines, he began reporting dreaming about explosions. Indeed, he was dreaming about an atomic bomb. Hearing this I wondered if he would now begin to bring more "anal" material to this analysis for another review, now with his integrated personality.

FOWLER: Hamilton has spent considerable time earlier in the analysis struggling with anal conflicts, and gaining some understanding of these dynamics. Can you explain why such a review occurred again and why now?

VOLKAN: Analysands review their problematic issues as they gain new internal structures and strengths. This way they resolve the internal conflicts in a better way with their newly gained strengths. Such reviews continue until such issues are no longer problematic or are shrunken. Thus, when I sensed that Hamilton would return to anal issues I did not consider it a failure in analysis; instead I considered it as a progressive move. By shrunken I mean this: Hamilton used to search for a perfect woman in his own city or in another city when an external situation increased his "need" and would spend days doing so. After he worked through this "need" he would think for half a day or even for half an hour about finding a perfect woman whom he "wished" to have and then his preoccupation would disappear. The problematic issues are even reviewed during the termination of an analysis when the analysand wants to say "good bye" to them.

One day he asked me if I knew that enemy submarines had killed eight thousand American sailors. He went on to state that the sailors were "sitting pigeons." I wondered out loud why he used the phrase "sitting pigeons" instead of the usual term "sitting ducks." A childhood memory came to his mind. He visualized a barn on the farm where he grew up. There were hundreds of pigeons nesting or flying around the barn. Little Hamilton would run after them and try to catch them. He recalled the pigeon droppings—pigeon "inky messes"—and experienced, on the couch, the smell associated with them. Suddenly he screamed: "I was the sitting pigeon on the potty trying to move my bowels. I was the sitting pigeon when they gave me enemas. I was the sitting pigeon when my father beat me." He fell asleep. His old symptom had returned. However, he woke up by himself after a few minutes and reported having many vague images, images that changed into submarines. Hamilton told me that now, submarines no longer symbolized penises, but stood for pieces of fecal material in the water. They were powerful, he said, and they were his rage and his defense against helplessness. Hamilton was owning his anal sadism.

Soon Hamilton became busy with a new business venture. This time he bought a textile factory some distance from Richmond, which needed repairing, refurbishing, and a new manager. I wondered if he was symbolically creating and refurbishing a new home representing his inner psychic structure. Since he gave me no associations to support or deny what came to my mind I said nothing. A rather beautiful woman in her late thirties was hired to manage the textile factory. Hamilton's thoughts about seducing this woman lasted only a few days. He reported to me that it was fine with him to have only a business relationship with this woman to whom he assigned the job of dealing with the workers at the new factory. Soon a fascinating psychic story developed concerning this textile factory that helped Hamilton master his conflicts connected to the "torture chamber" of his childhood.

FOWLER: Hamilton is moving from Oedipal concerns, to phallic, to anal, all in one session.

VOLKAN: He is revisiting these areas of conflict. It is as I described earlier—he moves forward, then backward. In this session he is working so hard! He is revisiting the areas in a creative way by using his interest in WWII as the symbolic material. He is now returning to the problems of his symbolized rage. Now he knows what the problem is—he is returning to the torture chamber where his father punished him for his rage. He recognizes how he thought of his feces as dangerous, explosive material. He realizes and thinks of himself as a sitting pigeon when they were giving him enemas, being beaten by his father. Now he wants to master the traumas and become his own man.

Hamilton hired some workers to build an office at the factory for him to use whenever he came to this location from Richmond. One day he was informed that his office was built and ready for inspection. Hamilton drove to the factory and was shocked when he visited his new office: the bathroom connected to this office was bigger than the office itself. The next week on the couch he spent most of his time planning how to "shrink" this bathroom. In the United States the word "shrink" is a typical nickname given to psychotherapists and psychoanalysts, and the psychoanalytic process itself is known as "shrinking a patient's head." As he planned to "shrink" the big bathroom, Hamilton was aware of his identification with his analyst. As he came up with different plans he would tell me, "I am working on my freedom by shrinking the big bathroom (torture chamber)."

While all this was happening, some bankers were giving him a hard time. He needed bankers' financial help to complete the repair and refurbishment of his new textile factory. As he planned to "shrink" the bathroom, he developed anxiety about meeting these bankers face-to-face. A thought occurred to him that they would "whip" him as his father had done. But in the midst of his anxiety, he managed to change the shape of the bathroom, "shrinking" it and making it appear "less oppressive." One day on the couch he told me, "I am a grown up man now. I do not need to wait at the bathroom door for my father to call me in. I can open the door and face him. He can no longer hurt me."

After this session he made an appointment with the bankers, faced them, and discussed his financial issues with them realistically. The bankers were impressed, and the meeting was most successful. The next day he brought the following dream:

> I was in Williamsburg, near the place where I was born. I saw this young man with blond hair. Yes, he was me. He looked like he was drunk. He fell down,

> and then he got up. Then he fell down again and got up again. He knew that he was going to die.

Without me saying anything, Hamilton told me that the young man who appeared drunk was his old self, complete with "craziness." His "crazy" part was dying. After waking up from the dream he thought of going to the run-down diner, the site of his old ritual, but instead he said to himself, "No need for me to go there." That same day he was going to a wedding in Maryland. "I am free," he realized and added, "I have no thoughts of taking a woman with me."

When he came to his next session he told me that after the session was over he was going to an Oriental rug store in downtown Charlottesville to buy a Turkish rug. In reality there was a colorful Turkish rug on my couch, which I liked very much and which was dominated by deep blue and decorated around the edges with bird motifs. Hamilton said that he was going to buy a Turkish rug with pastel colors and take it to his new office at the textile factory. I told him that pastel colors might represent a "tamed" Turkish analyst instead of a "terrible" Turkish analyst with a scimitar.

FOWLER: This appears to be a major shift in his mental life. He tells you that he is getting past his early traumas of the torture chamber.

VOLKAN: During his childhood he was very traumatized, as we had seen. Now he is going to shrink what had scared him so much when he was a child. How can he do this? Through further identification with the analyst. So the Turkish rug becomes a symbol that represents me as a new object (I am now symbolically a Soft Turk, no longer a Terrible Turk) and he takes me/rug with him to his new textile factory. Then he shrinks the torture chamber symbolically.

He laughed and told me that he had shrunk the bathroom, was killing his "crazy" self, and was taking me as a useful Turk with him symbolically to begin his life anew. For the first time since he started working with me, it occurred to him that his analysis might actually come to an end and he might lose me. He said that he might even learn how to mourn losing me. I knew that first he had to learn how to mourn losing his "crazy" self, truly own his new self and nurture his new self.

FOWLER: Hamilton is beginning to master the traumas. He reports a dream in which he is killing his crazy self. He is going to take you symbolically into his new life and realizes that his analysis may end. He said that he might learn how to mourn losing you. Then you realize that he is going to have to mourn his crazy self.

VOLKAN: Hamilton had not been capable of mourning because his internal world was split. His wife was dead for fifteen years and he continued to sleep with her ashes. He put Della's ashes in one room and kept another live woman in another. So there was no mourning, no capacity to mourn. As an adult Hamilton will learn to mourn, but only after he has become a cohesive person. He is going to mourn the blond crazy self. Can you imagine letting go of a part of your mind that has been your identity for fifty years? Another thing that we need to notice here: A person in his fifties can be analyzed.

Chapter 7
Finding and Letting Go a Warm Breast

During the latter part of the fourth year of his analysis Hamilton came to a Monday session the day after attending a wedding at an African-American church in Richmond. Recently, free from the parental influence of his childhood, he had begun enjoying his association with African-Americans, businessmen, technicians, and others who worked for his company and in his furniture, textile, and other factories. The day before this session, on Sunday, one of his assistant managers at the new factory, an African-American man, got married at the church. There was singing and Hamilton, now owning an integrated self-representation, joined the other guests in singing along.

After the wedding ceremony was over Hamilton drove to his oldest son's home nearby and played with one of his grandsons. The little boy pretended to be a rag doll on his grandfather's chest. Hamilton felt great joy and happiness playing with his grandson. At one point, his grandson pulled up his shirt and showed his naked tummy to this grandfather, smiling and wanting to be tickled. Hamilton sensed, seeing the little boy's tummy so soft and fat, that this grandson was well fed, happy, and without conflicts. No one would use Dr. Schreber's book as a guide to raise this little boy and no one would take him to a torture chamber. Hamilton felt good. He had "shrunken" the image of the "torture chamber" of his childhood and therefore he could now truly enjoy his grandson without envying the little boy for being treated—now and in the future—in a much better way than Hamilton had been as a child. In the middle of playing with his grandson Hamilton suddenly thought of his grandson as "Rolly Polly." This brought up the memory of a dog from his early childhood whose name was "Rolly Polly," and he recalled some images of playing with the dog. That night Hamilton was alone in his bed, reading a book, and when he slept he had a dream:

> I went to a church for black people. I looked up and saw a choir in the balcony singing and looking down at the sanctuary. Among the people in the balcony was James who in reality works at my new textile factory. In my dream James was the leader of the choir. He looked fatter, older, and motherly. He was singing passionately and broke into a sweat. He took his shirt off. His Rolly Polly chest was exposed, sweat covering his skin.

Without my saying anything Hamilton began interpreting his dream. He recalled having dreams of balconies during the first year of his analysis and my telling him that the balconies in his dreams represented the breasts of women. In these dreams he would go from one location to another looking up at different balconies, balconies that stood for the "nanas" to which he was "addicted." "So I know that the balcony in last night's dream above the sanctuary stood for a breast," Hamilton said. Then he added, "James with his Rolly Polly chest was a nipple. The passionate and joyful songs that came out of his mouth represented milk. I stood under the balcony taking in the milk. My dream is related to my nursing experience. I can almost recall nursing at my mother's breast. Yes, I now remember drinking from a bottle. It had a rubber nipple." After a brief silence Hamilton repeated, "It is so funny! I almost remember my mother's breast." I suggested to him that there might have been times when his mother was not depressed, but joyfully fed and loved him. "You might be remembering the most important thing that you had lost," I added.

Sitting behind him, I could see Hamilton blinking his eyes, which were filled with tears. He was experiencing sadness. I stopped talking so I would not disturb his sadness. After a while he summarized his "insight" once more, but this time his account was accompanied by appropriate and intense sadness. He lamented how all his life he had searched for the lost "good" mother/Abigail. He reported that the night he had the dream about the African-American church, he had no anxiety and no need to call a woman. He said that he enjoyed being alone reading a book. I talked to him about his finding a beautiful breast in a symbolic fashion in his dream and how he therefore no longer needed to carry out rituals nor expend enormous energy searching out others to find what it represented.

Hamilton came to his next session on Wednesday wearing a jogging suit and shoes. To do so, of course, was most unusual for him, but I said nothing. After lying on the couch he spoke about jogging and not finding time to change into his business suit before driving to Charlottesville to his session. I sensed that he was like a "baby," informally dressed, lying on my couch. Hamilton reported how he kept thinking about our previous session. He said that he was sure he was his mother's darling when she was not experiencing depression. As he was talking he moved his body about and this caused his jogging suit to rise up to his chest, exposing his naked tummy. He seemed not to be aware of this and kept talking. He was becoming "Rolly Polly" Hamilton, a breast. This amused me but I kept my feelings to myself.

FOWLER: You articulate that your job is to listen, enjoy and to be with him in the moment. I think that is very important, because earlier in the analytic process, you are much more active.

VOLKAN: Do you remember the earlier splitting transference, his having a second therapist, searching for a Turkish woman, compulsively defending against emotions? Now his splitting transference, and old compulsions are gone. During the initial phase of analysis, I had to be active in maintaining our therapeutic alliance, keeping a therapeutic frame, and dealing with his resistances. He is now in the middle phase of his analysis where the transference neurosis is at its peak, and where he is curious about what he brings to analysis and is able to do a great deal of self observation and where he is "playing" with the transference manifestations. Yes, I enjoyed seeing him doing so much analytic work.

Referring to his naked tummy, I told Hamilton that it was not clear in my mind who was nursing whom. Was I nursing him like a little baby on my couch, or was he nursing me like a Rolly Polly breast? I noted that who was nursing whom did not really matter. What mattered was his "bringing" a warm breast to my office, and the warm breast that he had lost decades ago when he was a baby was now between us. I told him that, furthermore, he had created this breast during his last dream. I emphasized that he now experientially and emotionally knew what the main loss of his childhood was. I added that once the image of a lost person or thing is internalized (as it appears in a dream) and/or it is created in the space between an analysand and the analyst, there is no need for the person to search compulsively through frantic actions for the lost person or thing in the outside world. At this point the individual realizes, I continued, what he or she wants to do with the internal image of the lost item. He or she has a choice to keep it or let it go, making it a memory.

VOLKAN: When a person successfully completes his or her mourning over a lost individual or thing, according to Veikko Tähkä (1984) the image of this lost individual or thing in the mourner's mind becomes a "futureless." A "futureless" image is not "hot" in the mourner's mind. The mourner does not use it (or its symbolic substitute in the environment) to gratify some of his or her wishes. A young man stops fantasizing that a wife who had been dead for some time will give him sexual pleasure, for example. Or, a woman stops wishing to boss her underlings at a job from which she had been fired years before. It can be said that we "bury" the object representation of a lost person or thing when we manage to make them futureless.

It took Hamilton two and a half months after his "finding" the lost warm breast in his dream and in the analytic office to fully understand my statement that he had a choice as to what to do with the image of an idealized breast. As we shall see, he made an "unconscious" choice to make it a memory, something gone forever, and to realize that there was no reason to frantically search for it. He reported the following dream:

> I was in an area of Charlottesville where blacks live. This area was changing color. I bought a home at this location but found out that a black woman was living there. In fact, she was living in a strange room. This room had a very strange shape.

Hamilton spoke about a section of Charlottesville that in actuality was "changing color." In the past this location was an all African-American residential area, but now many houses were being repaired and white-owned businesses were moving in. He then focused on the funny shape of the African-American woman's room in his dream, which reminded him of the horn shaped speaker of an old Victrola phonograph. When he was a small child his family owned such a phonograph. He loved to crank it up and listen to the famous Italian tenor Enrico Caruso sing. Suddenly Hamilton began to sing himself, something I had never heard him do before. Instead of singing an operatic aria like Caruso had, he began singing in dialect, the Negro song, "It ain't agwine to rain no more."

He seemed very regressed and in a trancelike state. I said nothing. He began to refer to black people as "niggers," as was customary in his childhood, but with affection. He reported that the black woman in the funnel-shaped room had gray hair and wore glasses. I thought that since I have gray hair (almost white) and wear glasses, I was condensed in the transference with this woman's image. Suddenly he recalled that the woman was the laundry woman who had worked for his family during his childhood. She was called "aunt" he said, and then he corrected himself. "No, only a real aunt was called 'aunt.' Old black women were called 'auntie.'" He murmured "Auntie no more." He was playing like a small child, "Auntie no more," "Ain't no more," imitating a black person's accent as he had done in his childhood. Suddenly he shouted "Abigail no more. Abigail is gone!" He realized that the black woman in the dream was Abigail's aunt, and he broke into song again:

> It ain't agwine to rain no more.
> How in the heck can I wash my neck?
> If it ain't agwine rain no more.
> Abigail isn't any more!

When his singing ended, Hamilton said in excitement that he could almost see the cabin where the woman in his dream who had gray hair, her husband, and Abigail actually had lived, and that he could almost smell the laundry tub. He saw the kitchen. "I have very clean images." He commented, "I can say good-bye to them. I can accept separations and losses, but I keep everyone and their memories united; good and bad are united." Needless to say this was a moving hour and it was fun for me to be present and observe Hamilton's working though some of his crucial childhood problems.

FOWLER: One of the deeply moving moments occurs when Hamilton starts to sing. Beautifully, he starts playing with the word "aunt" and ends up finding Abigail. In this moment, he discovers (at an emotional level) who he was looking for all this time. It is not just play, but deep insight with feeling.

VOLKAN: Internally, I become involved in the analytic work as if it is a play. Both the analysand and I play. The analysand, more than I, experiences pleasure, pain, "aha!" experiences during this play and I join him or her. The play is most serious.

Soon after this "learning" to turn the rediscovered warm breast into a "memory," Hamilton found peace in himself concerning his incestuous activities with Dorothy when he was a teenager. By now he was fully aware that his ejaculation on this sister's legs and tummy had more to do with his aggression concerning losing a "warm breast" than his having sexual feelings toward her. He had intertwined his aggression with sex.

In his daily routine Hamilton was becoming a good father. It was as if he was given a second chance to treat his children with affection and be close to them. However, his relationship with his siblings had improved only slightly.

They were all on speaking terms, but they were not close. Hamilton sensed that his siblings themselves were not interested in closeness.

At one infrequent family gathering at his brother's house, Hamilton asked to be excused early. Dorothy, who was now in her fifties and married, had come to Virginia for the family gathering. She asked him, "Where are you going now?" and Hamilton believed he knew what she meant. In Hamilton's mind his sister was implying that he was leaving the family gathering early in order to chase some women. He felt badly that his sister had not yet realized how much he had changed. He found himself spontaneously and seriously responding to Dorothy, "I am going to my home and I will pray." He expressed this in a tone that indicated he was not lying and that indeed, he planned to do what he had said he was going to do.

On the way home, Hamilton realized that through his spontaneous sincere response to his sister, he was indirectly asking for forgiveness. On the couch, telling me this incident, he appeared sad. As I already stated, he and Dorothy had never spoken openly about what had taken place between them decades earlier, and as an adult he always felt awkward around her. He imagined that she remained angry with him throughout their adult lives. He told me that by way of his reply to his sister's question as he was leaving the family gathering, he was telling her that he had changed, he had stopped chasing women, including her, and that he would pray for forgiveness.

When Hamilton came to his next session he reported that the day before he had received an unexpected telephone call from Dorothy. She had already left Virginia and was at her own home in Georgia, and on the telephone she was warm and friendly. She surprised him greatly by telling him that she had an important item, a box that she wanted to give him. She went on to say that she had had this box for years and had taken it from their parents' home after their deaths. This box contained Hamilton's school records from elementary through high school. It also included newspaper clippings about Hamilton's activities in school sports. It was clear that it was their mother who had collected and saved these items about her son, because in the box there were also letters written to her by relatives. It appeared that his mother saved these letters in which there were statements praising Hamilton. Hamilton, who had not known of the existence of this box and its contents, was moved. He realized that his mother who "rejected" him, who punished him and who could not demonstrate her love to him openly, secretly kept mementos about him and did, in fact, love him.

Hamilton spent considerable time on the couch speaking about this box and why Dorothy had kept it from him through the years. I mostly stayed silent and listened. He came to the conclusion that, since his sister had been angry with him, she had not wanted him to know, until now, that his mother loved him. Following his "apology" as he was leaving the latest family gathering, which told her indirectly that he had changed, Hamilton felt that Dorothy forgave him. A few days later the box arrived at Hamilton's house. On the couch Hamilton expressed a great sense of relief. Although he and his sister would never openly discuss what had happened between them, and they never developed a close relationship, after Hamilton received the box they remained friendly in a comfortable way.

Chapter 8
Why Did Atatürk Encourage Turkish Women to Remove Their Veils?

At the beginning of his psychoanalysis, Hamilton described his incestuous-like activities. Ejaculating on Dorothy's legs and tummy as an early teen and having sex with his sister-in-law and step-mother-in-law when he was an adult were primarily related to his childhood aggression toward his mother who was depressed and who deprived him of her love, and his wish to replace the depressed mother (as well as lost Abigail) with an idealized woman and be her only darling. To a lesser extent, these activities expressed derivatives of his unexpressed Oedipal wishes. During the early part of his fourth year of treatment, Hamilton was involved in a primitive (not fully symbolized) form of Oedipal activity—a drama between a father, a mother, and a son who competes with the father in possessing the mother—when he joined a couple in their bed and compared his penis with the erect penis of the other man while fantasizing about the size of my genital organ. Toward the end of the fourth year of his analysis, his Oedipal concerns became more sophisticated, more symbolic, and began to appear in the therapeutic stories he placed between us. In "normal" child development, a little boy who emotionally struggles with his father for his mother's love and who competes with the older man eventually identifies with the older man as part of the process of "learning" how to become a man himself. This is how a little boy resolves his Oedipus complex: instead of fighting with daddy, he joins daddy through identification. He then lets his father have his mother and feels free to find his own woman when he grows up, just like his father did. In analysis the resolution of unfinished Oedipal issues or, as it was in Hamilton's case, going through the oedipal phase for the first time with a mended self, are accompanied by several things: the analysand's competition with his analyst for a woman, his identification with the analyst as a man, and eventually his feeling comfortable with having "two men" in the analyst's office who can now have "man to man" communications while still examining the analysand's unfinished and/or conflicting psychological problems.

Toward the end of the fourth year of his analysis, Hamilton visited some friends in Charlottesville and all together they went to see a play. Two days later he reported seeing me at the theater sitting next to an obese woman, and he thought that the obese woman was my wife. I had not seen him when I was at the theater. The night after going to the theater, Hamilton dreamt of a man and a woman but he could not recognize them. Hamilton himself was in the dream trying to tell a "joke" to this man. In giving free association to his dream he recalled how his father loved "to trade horses." Once his father played a "joke" on one of his friends. He groomed an old horse to make the animal look younger and healthier and sold this horse to his friend. The buyer later realized how Hamilton's father had tricked him, but both men were good-natured about the event and laughed about it. Hamilton recalled how his father loved telling this story again and again.

Hamilton went on to remember having sex with an obese woman ten years earlier, although his relationship with her was rather short lived. He encouraged this woman to lose weight and even brought her to a Weight Watcher's program and paid her fee to participate. But when the woman lost weight and looked much better and sexier, she fell in love with another man and married him, leaving Hamilton.

After reporting this story, Hamilton began berating me for not having a slender woman. He wanted to "educate" me as to how I could turn my obese woman into a better-looking woman. I asked Hamilton what "my" woman would do after she became slender. Would she leave me then, as his obese woman had done when she became slender? Hamilton began to laugh and said that if "my" woman became slender and sexy he could take her from me. I reminded him that his father had made a horse look better and sold it to his friend, but it was really a joke. We needed to look at this "horse trading" more carefully so we could better understand what we were trading.

Hamilton told me another event and another dream to further illuminate what was happening in his mental life concerning two men competing for one woman. He had been to a dinner party where he sat next to a sexy and slender woman, Charlotte, the wife of a President and CEO of a business that was bigger than Hamilton's business. The dinner party was given to honor this man, who was addressed as "The President" (a symbolic father figure). Hamilton told me that if his old self were still present he would probably have flirted with Charlotte. But, at the dinner party, instead of doing this, he and Charlotte ended up having a serious discussion about the U.S. Supreme Court and some of its recent decisions. While talking with Charlotte he had penile sensation and at one point his penis was erect. In spite of this, he continued their discussion about the Supreme Court and felt rather comfortable. That night he had a dream in which he was jogging with Charlotte, but he felt embarrassed because he knew that she was someone else's wife. He jumped up as if defying gravity and landed on the seat of a bulldozer that had a huge steam shovel attached to it. He felt that the steam shovel was between his legs.

The steam shovel was his erect penis, he said. But, it was funny that he had combined his sexual impulse with a discussion about the Supreme Court, which, among other things, judges people's activities. I sensed that Hamilton, in a symbolic way, was bringing what psychoanalysts call "id impulses" (his erection) together with "superego" (supreme court), which attempts to tame "id" impulses.

Soon afterwards, I began hearing about Hamilton's befriending a couple in their eighties. According to Hamilton, the couple was still in love. Hamilton knew that he was going out with them in order to "learn" how to be around a "loving couple" that accepted him and approved of him as a "younger man." Hamilton said that his own age was advancing and when he reached his eighties he hoped to be like his new friend, this older man. He was sad that he had lived so many years without experiencing mature love for a woman. I felt for him and told him that unfortunately he had no choice but to be philosophical about his "lost years" and focus on his present and future life.

Hamilton was filled with memories of his life with Della, his first wife. They had children and a beautiful house. At that time there was another woman in his life who was in her eighties. Their "friendship" began when Hamilton was briefly involved in a business deal with this woman and benefited greatly from it. He now recalled having a fantasy that with the money he had received from her he would buy a beautiful farm where he would watch "rainbows." In reality, this woman was overbearing. Hamilton described how she looked like Dolly and, in fact, stood for Dolly. Hamilton became this woman's "slave" and obeyed her "orders" to do this or that, causing him to neglect Della, thereby hurting her. Telling this story brought tears to Hamilton's eyes. "I have a sense of remorse now," he said. "I'm sorry for what I did to Della. I wish I had been a better husband."

His new friends in their eighties were concrete symbols of good parents. Hamilton said that they were "constantly" nice and respectful as they related to each other and to him. Then he addressed me. "You are constant too; you are like my best friend in the whole world." Then he recalled another devastating event in his life when he was a teenager that had spoiled his identification with a "good" Oedipal father. What came to his mind was another horse. This time the horse was a good and strong one that needed no grooming to look younger in order to be sold. When Hamilton was in his early teens, his older brother left the farm to go to college. Hamilton recalled how he then hoped that now, with his brother away, his father would pay attention to him and "bond" with him. While his father "whipped" both sons when they were younger, Hamilton sensed that his brother was his father's favorite son. When his brother left for college his father bought Hamilton a beautiful horse. Hamilton was delighted and secretly hoped to leave his troubles from his earlier years behind him, become his father's companion, and be like the older man. One day, his horse ate some green apples, its tummy bloated, and it died, taking away the link (the horse) that connected him to a "good," loving father. Hamilton now, on my couch, openly grieved for his beautiful horse (also symbolizing his father's approval of his manhood), for losing an opportunity to be his father's friend, and for losing so many years without a comfortable relationship with a woman of his choice.

Unfortunately, while reviewing his disappointment over his attempt to be close to a "good" father, once more I left him for two weeks. When we got together again and he settled on the couch he said, "This time, when you were away, I looked for terrible Turks with scimitars, but I could not find any. Instead I did a great deal of self-observation when you were gone." While I was away, accepting an invitation, he had gone to South Carolina to visit his friend David, whom he had known for decades. David was Hamilton's age and also very rich. When Hamilton saw David again after some years apart, he realized that David had had a surgical face-lift and now dyed his hair. David also informed Hamilton that he was taking medication to help him achieve penile erection. David owned a yacht with an all-woman crew, even the captain. David "created" a world where his illusion of being the only darling of multiple women had come true, bringing to reality, Hamilton realized, his own former desires. But he also observed that this "world" created by an elderly man playing the role of darling to multiple women was funny, a caricature of an infantile dream. Hamilton said: "I did not think that I was jealous of David, but then I realized that I might be, because one night alone in my bed in South Carolina, I felt my old depression. But then I recognized its origin." He added: "My depression was lifted. The solution is not to find a perfect woman. Indeed, I am no longer concerned with finding a perfect woman."

At this time Hamilton was dating Lisa on and off. Lisa was in her forties and a widow. They were not in love, but friends who would often sleep together. Lisa's parents were alcoholics and Lisa would tell Hamilton not to drink wine when they went to a restaurant. At first Hamilton felt irritated, but then he felt more comfortable when he understood why Lisa tried to interfere with his social drinking. He considered it "her problem." Thus, he continued to enjoy his wine at restaurants, not letting her problem contaminate his internal world.

I listened without much comment to his observations about what happened during my absence. Since I was no longer a Turk with a scimitar sitting behind him, Hamilton talked in a lively manner, sharing his excitement about changes he saw in himself. He told me that when I was away he found some old volumes of *National Geographic* magazine dating from 1928 to 1940. He noted that there were many articles in these volumes on the Turks and Turkey (symbolically the analyst), and he read them all. They led Hamilton to research further and he found books that taught him more about the collapse of the Ottoman Empire and the birth of the Modern Turkish Republic after World War I. He told me that he had learned how Turks managed to change many old traditions after they founded their republic. He now knew that Turks changed their alphabet, giving up Arabic script and replacing it with Latin script. He also knew that they became secular, trading Islamic Law for a legal system based on those of some European countries. He learned to appreciate the role Kemal Atatürk, the founder of modern Turkey, played in leading the Turkish revolution. He understood that Atatürk got rid of the "bad" Ottoman Sultan (representing Hamilton's "bad" father figure) and replaced him as the Turks' new "father." Hamilton was especially fascinated by Atatürk's encouraging the Turkish women to give up their veils, and he wondered why Atatürk wanted the Turkish women's faces uncovered so they could be seen by others.

FOWLER: Hamilton is now working on Oedipal issue and problems of the superego. When he tells you of the good Turkish leader getting rid of the bad Sultan and freeing the women from an oppressive control, it is easy to hear the symbolic link to his changing experience of his oppressive superego and his wish to be a better man to women.

VOLKAN: He is telling me, and himself, that he can do this. If Turks can be free of a symbolic bad father, then he can do it too. I am no longer a Turk with a scimitar, but a revolutionary Turk. He will identify with the latter and change his internal world and develop a more benign and more idealized superego. But this does not mean that he will not review some more Oedipal problems with his original Hitler-like father image. Reviews are necessary until new structures are settled in him.

Some years before Hamilton became my analysand, my friend, Princeton historian Norman Itzkowitz, and I wrote an extensive psychobiography on Atatürk (Volkan and Itzkowitz, 1984). Accordingly, I thought I knew a great deal about this Turkish leader's internal motivations that pushed him not only to be a military leader, but also a revolutionary one. It was clear to me that in his "study" of the Turks during my two-week absence, Hamilton had not come across our book. In spite of my narcissistic temptation to tell him about my "expertise" concerning Atatürk's life, I refrained from doing so. During our separation, instead of searching for a Turkish woman or a "perfect" woman, Hamilton this time wanted to create the image of a Turkish man with whom to identify. He was, at this point in his treatment, less preoccupied with finding his mother's "breast" than he was involved in finding an effective Oedipal father.

I told him that when a woman is no longer hidden behind a veil she is no longer mysterious or powerful. "You can see her as she is," I added. I explained to him that his concept of "perfection" was like a veil. When his women "wore" his "perfection," they became powerful; they could make or break him. I suggested that Hamilton himself was able to remove the veil of his "perfect" women. Now he could see women as they were and he could relate to them realistically.

I knew that in his transference relationship with me, I was becoming more and more a "good" Oedipal father. It was as if I were his Atatürk, revolutionizing his internal world. I sensed, however, that his old images of the "whipping" father and corresponding "traumatized child" were not altogether gone, and he externalized these images onto others. Since I did not yet know what he would do with these externalized images and how and when he would bring them back to us for a closer look, I said nothing about them. In his sessions, just at the completion of four years of his analysis, Hamilton evolved then President George H. Bush's image into the "whipping father" and the Jews during Nazi Germany as the "tortured child." He began to re-examine his childhood once more by referring to a current and a historical event: the brewing troubles in the Persian Gulf region and Nazi Germany. But, he was going to carry out this examination with a self that, since its mending, had evolved. His self now included ongoing identifications with his analyst as a person who was different from his childhood whipping Oedipal father. But, he was not confident that the analyst would remain this way. Hamilton would, at times, still contaminate the analyst's new image with the fear-inducing images of his childhood.

Chapter 9
Joining the Man's World

After the invasion of Kuwait by Iraq, Saddam Hussein, then the President of Iraq, declared Kuwait the ninetieth Province of Iraq on August 2, 1990. The American government under President George H. Bush anticipated that Iraq also intended to invade Saudi Arabia. On August 6 "Operation Desert Shield" began when, at the Saudi's request, Bush ordered U.S. troops deployed to protect Saudi Arabia. Hamilton began to speak about President Bush on the couch in early fall, 1990. He found the President's views about Iraq and the Middle East frightening, and he was worried that President Bush would commit the U.S. to war. Hamilton, like everyone else, was bombarded by repetitious daily news about what was going on in Iraq, Kuwait, Saudi Arabia, Palestine, and Israel. I sensed that bringing political issues to the couch also had something to do with his identification with me. At the time, as I already stated, I was the Director of the Center for the Study of Mind and Human Interaction at the University of Virginia. This Center's task was to study the psychology of large ethnic, religious or national groups and international relationships. Once Hamilton saw me on television where I was briefly interviewed about developing international events, and thus he learned something about my professional activities outside of the purely medical and psychoanalytic ones.

For an analysand, seeing his or her psychoanalyst outside the analyst's office and receiving information about the analyst from outside sources always induces transference manifestations. When the analysand brings the external event about the analyst to his or her sessions this, of course, is examined. Then the transference distortions are corrected and/or included in the ongoing therapeutic play between the analysand and the psychoanalyst. There are occasions when this outside information complicates matters: it can interfere with how the analysand relates to his or her psychoanalyst, whether it be as an oral mother, Oedipal father, or other transference figures. So traditionally psychoanalysts try to live a life away from their analysands' external environments and they shy away from public appearances. Of course, this is an impossible task, especially if a psychoanalyst, like myself, lives in a relatively small city like Charlottesville and is a university professor whose profession includes public speeches.

By this time in his analysis, I perceived that Hamilton was not a deeply religious person. He was involved in traditions of his religious background, celebrated Christmas, and usually he would go to Sunday church services. Certainly, he was not at all a religious fanatic. This induced no complicated reaction from me since I am also a person who is not concerned with religious beliefs or practices. Meanwhile, until this time I also had no clear idea about Hamilton's political orientation. But "Operation Desert Shield," combined with his seeing me interviewed on television, changed things. From the fall of 1990 until early 1991 when the Gulf War ended, now in the fifth year of his psychoanalysis, Hamilton frequently spoke about political issues. I avoided discussing his political views in their own right, referring to them only when they became a stage upon which his internal issues were reenacted. Even then, I mainly focused on what was being enacted and not on external events as they concerned others. It turned out that most of his ideas and feelings about wars and war-like conditions were similar to mine. This, of course, helped me avoid unnecessary personal reactions to his views, although if I had such reactions, I am sure, my training as a psychoanalyst and my clinical experience would still have allowed me to remain in a therapeutic position.

FOWLER: With the building conflict in Iraq and Kuwait, such tensions on a global scale, I imagine it would be difficult to contain personal reactions. You are an analyst, but you are also a citizen who can become inflamed by the politics of war. Despite your second profession, you make a clear point of not bringing your opinion into the session.

VOLKAN: If I discuss politics directly with my analysand or my "second profession" I may come close to managing his life since he will respond to my political views as resembling his or her views or being opposites. My focus is on the analysand's internal world and on how external events become intertwined with his internal processes. The analysand may sense my political sentiments and may react to them, but this is different than bringing my political opinions to the sessions directly.

As President Bush continued amassing troops in the Persian Gulf, Hamilton's images of his "whipping father," now mainly projected onto the President, were reactivated. He had a dream in which President Bush appeared in a bathroom. But this time the story of the dream did not follow his usual storyline of being "whipped" by a symbolic father in a bathroom. Instead, in this dream, President Bush took out his penis and the dreaming Hamilton noticed that the President's penis was no different than his own. Hamilton, in a sense, was "daring" to have the same size penis as his dangerous "father" had.

His associations to this dream indicated that he "shrunk" his father's penis like he had "shrunk" his childhood "torture chamber" when he modified the bathroom next to his new textile factory office. Hamilton, speaking about his dream, recalled an incident from his high school days. He was given the task of inviting a well-known local person to be a guest speaker at his school. As soon as I heard this I sensed that he was, in the transference, referring to me, since I was a "guest speaker" on a television show, but in order to allow his story to develop, I did not immediately tell him what came to my mind. Hamilton continued to describe how, although this man asked for a thousand dollars as a speaking fee, Hamilton was able to persuade him to give the speech for only eight hundred. When he reported his success in saving money for the school to one of his teachers, the teacher replied: "You Jewed him (the speaker) down." Hamilton recalled how he did not like hearing his teacher make a racist remark.

Hamilton then tried to go on to another topic, but I asked him to stay with his story.

He recalled how his father used to say that he enjoyed "bargaining" with Jewish businessmen; "Jews bargain instead of setting prices," his father used to say. Hamilton now wondered if what his father said was true. He wanted to focus on cultural differences and understand how people from different cultures and/or religions typically express themselves when interacting with one another. Instead of telling him that his remarks might refer to us as well (one FFV American and one Turkish-American), I wanted him to continue and evolve his story in his own way. He went back to President Bush and used unflattering expressions to describe him. He was downsizing the President. The image of the President on television, he said, reminded him of a man named Oliver who was then seventy-five years old. Hamilton added with laughter, "Everyone knows that Oliver had a penis implant." Soon Hamilton experienced some anxiety. On the surface, he was shrinking President Bush's/the analyst's penis (or giving them an artificial penis) and thus he was achieving equality with his symbolic father figures or even surpassing them. He was "Jewing them down." But, underneath his "success" was his identification with victims, the Jews. His "resolution" of his Oedipus complex was not yet a true one. On the surface, he could compete and even become better than his father, but secretly he would remain someone whose "fate" was to be victimized.

Hamilton opened one of his sessions by projecting a victim image to me, asking out loud, "Are you Jewish?" I gave no answer. He said that he knew I was Turkish, but I might be a Turkish Jew. I told him that if I were a Turkish Jew then I could "Jew him down" and downsize his penis. Meanwhile, he reported playing tennis with the nice older gentleman of Turkish origin whom both of us knew, although this man did not know that Hamilton was my analysand. Psychologically speaking, he continued to have a friendly association with the Turkish psychoanalyst and identify with him while he also used his analyst as a target of his, still existing, victimized self, and as one who could still punish him.

I had the habit of buying small mementoes from different countries that I had visited during the years I was involved in unofficial diplomacy. I had a miniature metal sphinx from Egypt, a small painted cow's collar with a bell from Switzerland, and a Lenin medallion from the Soviet Union, for example. My bookshelf covered the entire wall in front of my psychoanalytic couch. For over four years Hamilton had seen my collection and paid no special attention to it, but while his hours were filled with references to President Bush and Saddam Hussein, Hamilton began showing interest in these small items. I noted that now, when he got up from my couch after a session, he would stop for a few seconds in front of my bookshelf and look at my collection before opening the door and leaving my office. I would continue sitting in my comfortable chair behind the couch until he left.

One day he opened his session by reporting a dream. In his dream he saw a giant smoke stack with fire and smoke coming out of it. He was in a field in front of the building with the smoke stack, wheeling Mary in a baby carriage through snow, dirt and feces. The smoke stack reminded him of chimneys of a Nazi concentration camp, and Mary in the baby carriage looked like the corpse of a Jew ready to be incinerated by the Nazis. A few days earlier, Hamilton reported to me how Mary's lawyer was trying to force Hamilton's lawyer to get more money for her. The financial aspect of the divorce was not yet settled. "It is no wonder that I made Mary a victim in my dream. I am angry with her," Hamilton remarked.

At this point Hamilton lifted up his head a little bit from the pillow on my couch and looked intently toward my collection of memorabilia on the shelf. "Aha!" he said with some anxiety and excitement. "There is my dream!" And he raised his right hand and pointed at an item. It took me a few seconds to realize what he was pointing at—an emblem of Ben Gurion University in Israel. The emblem, painted gold, was encased in transparent plastic on a wooden stand. The entire item was about four inches by three inches. It was a gift to me from General Shlomo Gazit, the well-known Israeli general who once was in charge of Israeli military intelligence and who was a participant in the unofficial Arab-Israeli dialogue series that took place from 1979 to 1986. This series of meetings, which had the blessing of the Israeli, Egyptian, and American governments, was sponsored by the American Psychiatric Association's Committee on Foreign Affairs (Volkan, 1988). I participated in all these meetings for six years and for the last three, I was in charge of the facilitating team. General Gazit, who at the time was the President of Ben Gurion University, had given me the emblem at one of these meetings. I did not tell Hamilton how I got this item. Now looking at the Ben Gurion University emblem I could see that it looked like a flame. Hamilton reported that the emblem looked like a volcano (psychoanalyst "Volkan"). I was the smoke stack in the dream; I was the Nazi father. I told Hamilton that Nazis and Jews, the torturers, and tortured, these dichotomies were now created between us. In his experience, I was a Jew, but I was also Hitler; furthermore, he was a Jew and was also a Nazi.

Once more, I became aware of how mental images of Nazis and the Holocaust had become a universal symbol for extreme aggression and extreme pain (Volkan, Ast & Greer, 2002). Now both "Hitler" and the "Jew" were in my office. I thought he could "play" with these identities and tame his extreme aggression and shame even more. Indeed, Hamilton "played" with the "items" on my shelf without my telling him to do so. During the sessions that followed, he still made references to Saddam Hussein and President Bush, but would then quickly turn his focus to the items on my shelf. Some items, in his mind, also became sexual organs. For example, he insisted that the small metal sphinx was a symbol of my penis. Meanwhile, he kept reading editorials from various newspapers and spoke on the couch about which writers were for and which were against war. The approaching war that was threatening the outside world was reflected by a war within him. He had repeated dreams about "windmills." This brought to his mind the image of himself as Don Quixote, transferring his internal fears to "windmills" and then fighting with them. He also dreamed of wearing a "crown"—becoming a man and symbolic "father" himself.

One day he did something most unusual in the middle of a session. He got up from the couch, walked to my bookshelf, looked closely at my "memorabilia," and then touched them, especially the metal sphinx that he held in his palm for a few seconds. I thought that, through this action within the analytic office, he had made a symbolic but concrete contact with extreme aggression, extreme pain, and my "penis" which, in his mind, personified such feelings. I said nothing, but wondered if he would become anxious or have homosexual panic. This did not happen. Instead, he returned to the couch and exhibited no anxiety but looked like a shy young man and said to me, "I know that you run this hospital (Blue Ridge Hospital) and you travel. Tell me about your work. Tell me how you work. Who are you?" I told him that for over four years now he had experiences with me, and accordingly, he already knew me! I replied that his knowing me this way, within our analytic work, was much better and more important than my telling him about my other activities.

FOWLER: Can you expand on the importance of Hamilton physically touching the symbols in your office?

VOLKAN: Now Hamilton is revisiting the fears of a dangerous father as he attempts to overcome the re-emerging fears that are stimulated by a threat of an external war. As he works through these fears, he castrates me symbolically and therefore he expects retaliation on my part. Then he does something remarkable—he touches my symbolic penis. This is a most unusual event and I say nothing. This time he tries to overcome the early childhood traumas by an action! Hamilton is like a kid at the zoo who is afraid of a camel's big mouth and his long neck. He is afraid until he touches the camel. Once he touches the "camel" he relaxes and laughs. The fear turns to excitement because he now knows that the camel is a non-biting camel and that he will not be hurt. His fantasy of a dangerous camel was just a fantasy and a fantasy is different than a reality. It is useful to once again revisit the concept of unconscious fantasy and especially its "actualized" form. "Actualization" of an unconscious fantasy occurs when the child's external-world experiences interfere with the usual restriction of fantasy only or mostly to the psychological realm due to trauma. Consider a little girl at the time she is developing unconscious oedipal sexual fantasies about her father: such unconscious fantasies, in a routine developmental process, stay within the psychological realm; using them to satisfy infantile sexual desires, to accompany masturbatory activities, to enhance self-esteem, to create "bad" competitor-mother images, for example. They simply remain as a set of psychological processes subject to modification as the child ascends the developmental ladder. If this little girl is sexually molested during the Oedipal phase by her father or by his substitute, however, her unconscious Oedipal fantasy becomes "actualized": because there is a strong link between the uncon-

scious fantasy and reality, the little girl's unconscious fantasy will exist in both the psychological and experiential realms. In contrast, the little boy who passively and briefly witnessed a primal scene is unlikely to "actualize" his unconscious fantasy; for a fantasy to be "actualized," the child's involvement in the actual experience that initiates it must be unusually severe and/or repetitive.

Some individuals with childhood experiences of severe bodily injuries, surgeries, near-death experiences, early object losses accompanied with other traumatic experiences, or exposure to massive destruction (e.g., earthquake or war) are prone to developing "actualized" unconscious fantasies. A child who actually survives an earthquake, for example, may link that experience to a sexual or aggressive fantasy—developing, for example, a repressed "story line" to the effect that, if he or she does not submit to the superego, his or her aggression may cause catastrophe. In fact, Bergmann (1982), Kogan (1998, 2000), and Volkan, Ast, and Greer (2002) have illustrated that a child may also develop "actualized" (Bergmann and Kogan use the term "concretized") unconscious fantasies as a result of identifying with parents or other relatives—or, indeed, with the large group (i.e., ethnic, religious, or national group) with which the child is associated—who have sustained massively traumatic experiences, such as surviving the Holocaust. In this situation, trauma survivors "deposit" (Volkan, 1987) their injured images, with associated affects and representations of historical events, into the self-representations of their offspring, imparting to the subsequent generation(s) psychological tasks (e.g., mourning, reversing helplessness) that properly belong to the generation directly traumatized.

Sexual or aggressive assault, acute and repeated sexual or aggressive stimulation by parents or siblings also may actualize a child's fantasy. For example his experiences in the "torture chamber" I believe actualized Hamilton's unconscious fantasy that feces is a powerful destructive tool and that the unconscious fantasy that homosexual assault and castration by a father actually is possible.

There are those who are opposed to introducing the category of "actualized" unconscious fantasies because classical psychoanalysis considers only the realm of "psychic reality"; classical psychoanalytic technique would thus render superfluous any concept that addresses difficulties in keeping mental content restricted to the psychic realm. Nevertheless, I note in practice that the reactivation of certain unconscious fantasies within the transference-countertransference axis complicates classical technique by creating specific problems that cannot be successfully negotiated without referring to the world beyond the analysand's psychic reality. If a person with an "actualized" unconscious fantasy enters into psychoanalysis as an adult, and if the "story line" of the fantasy becomes available to him or her, that individual may have difficulty differentiating where his or her (now conscious) fantasy ends and where reality begins. For this person, then, keeping the "hot" transference limited to the psychological realm will be difficult. Indeed, patients who possess actualized unconscious fantasies experience a general blurring of reality testing when their fantasies are reactivated. Such patients experience symbols or objects of displacement representing various aspects of the actualized unconscious fantasies as "protosymbols" (Werner and Kaplan, 1963): to the patient, that is to say, they are what in actuality they represent. For example, such a patient experiences a cave not as if it could be his mother's belly, but as his mother's belly. Another experiences the neighbors as being Nazis, not as being like Nazis. On an intellectual level, the patient can "hear" his or her analyst's interpretation of the protosymbols' meaning, but the interpretation alone is insufficient for the patient to free himself or herself from using symbols or objects of displacement as protosymbols. Such a patient's therapeutic regression needs to take him or her to the point(s) at which the unconscious fantasy became "actualized" in order for the process of "therapeutic regression followed by therapeutic progression" to be successful. In a sense, the patient must "go back" to the moment(s) at which mental content and external reality originally converged in order to re-establish the difference between what belongs to an unconscious fantasy and what belongs to the external world. In psychoanalytic treatment, I believe, these patients need to be involved in "therapeutic play" in order to re-establish sound reality testing. Hamilton, as we had observed, was involved in therapeutic plays. Here, within the session, he took an unusual action and touched the analyst's symbolic penis. I think this too was in the service of making his actualized unconscious fantasy a routine one that belongs only to a psychological realm.

The session ended. That night Hamilton had a dream and reported it to me the next day:

> There were two two-story houses, one next to the other. They were almost identical, but one was white and the other one gray. The gray one had a site violation, part of it was built over a border.

Hamilton right away knew that the houses represented the two of us. I was the "White House" (President Bush/father figure). "Besides," he said, "your hair is white." He was the "gray" one with an integrated self. He was no longer "skimpy" and no longer needed to be watched over.

I brought up his "boundary violation" the day before when he got up from the couch and touched my items. He declared that his action did not make him anxious. He wanted a "concrete" contact with me, to test me in order to experience, once and for all, if I was or was not like his original (Oedipal) father. He touched me (my items) and proved to himself that I was not Hitler. I did not burn him, but remained in my analytic position, curious. After the last session, before he had his dream, he and his girl friend, Lisa, played tennis with the older gentleman of Turkish origin and his wife. Now Hamilton told me freely that he was a better tennis player than the Turkish man. At one point, the older man jokingly said, "Let's get revenge!" and suggested that he and Hamilton play against his wife and Lisa. The two men joined forces against the two women, and the men won the tennis match. I told Hamilton that the "boundary violation" in his dream might also refer to another boundary crossed within himself: can he leave his childhood's way of relating to older men or men in general, and freely team up with and join a man's world? Upon hearing this, Hamilton began to wonder more about me. He realized that I was very different from his childhood father. One day he came with a mental list of my qualifications and told me about his list. He liked that I showed constancy. He said I was "even tempered, intelligent, good humored, and was interested in the world." He found out where I lived and he thought that this was good, since he liked that section of Charlottesville. But, he added, there were things about me that he did not like. He did not like that I had an old car. He added that if the fat woman he had seen in the theatre was my wife, he would like for me to have a sexier woman. I was certainly and more clearly becoming what psychoanalysts call a "new object" in his mind. But, he also realized that he was still relating to me as if I were Hitler (torturing father) and a Jew (the tortured child Hamilton who was projected into me). But he could "play" with such images of me now, instead of feeling much anxiety. He attempted to integrate my "Hitler" and "Jewish" identities by declaring, "Hitler had Jewish blood!"

The next session when he came back, his "play" of integrating me continued. Instead of going to the couch directly, he inspected my metal sphinx once more, this time without touching it and then examined a painting of flowers on my office wall. After lying on my couch, he kept repeating "penises" and "flowers," "aggression and love," "linking them or not linking them."

After this session, during a weekend, another "two-birthdays together" event occurred, and, once more, Hamilton gave a party to celebrate the event. This time he had no need to go to another state, find a woman, and repeat the illusion of being his "mother's" only child. But, when he came to his Monday session and reported an uneventful, and in fact, a most pleasant "two birthdays together" event, he suddenly realized that he had put on, "by mistake," a blue jacket and black trousers. This puzzled him. This time instead of the "penises" and "flowers" preoccupation, he became preoccupied with "black and blue." I told Hamilton that in the past, remembering his younger siblings' births and his losing his mother induced his rage and murderous fantasies. In turn, he would expect punishment. I explained to him that now such feelings were tamed and/or effectively repressed. Accordingly, his expectation of punishment would only appear in a symbolic form. I told him that "black and blue" most likely symbolically referred to a battered child whose skin turned "black and blue" from whippings. He replied that this could be true, since he was surprised that he did not want to come to his session that morning.

On another day before our session, Hamilton looked closely at pictures in the small hallway leading to my office. In the hallway there was also a huge picture of Sigmund Freud with a cigar in his hand. Hamilton reported, "I looked at Freud. I thought he looked a little sad. Then I thought it was I who was sad." He stopped talking and actually looked sad. Then suddenly, in an animated way, he told me a joke. This was the first time he had done this, and on one level, I knew that he wanted to join the man's world and could now bring himself to share a joke with another man. He was also identifying with his father, the father who was not scary but enjoyed telling jokes. Here is his joke:

> There is a ninety-four-year-old man sitting on a bench crying. Another man who happens to be passing by stops and asks the older man the reason for his being sad and upset. The ninety-four-year-old man answers: "You see, I am married to a beautiful twenty-four-year-old woman. It is not a crime. She is such a good cook, she is such a good sex partner in bed." He stops and now really begins to sob. The other man is puzzled and says: "You are so lucky to have such a woman. I don't understand your distress." The ninety-four-year-old man now screams with pain: "You see, I do not remember our home's address. I cannot find my woman."

When he finished telling his joke and chuckling about it, I told him that his sadness was due to losing his "idealized perfect woman." She had become only a memory. He agreed.

Soon Hamilton became involved in many civic activities in Richmond. This brought him in contact with various high-level state government people, including a prestigious African-American man. Hamilton enjoyed his association with these men and especially the interaction with the African-American individual. He thought of Morris, Abigail's brother, and felt good that he could now have a man-to-man relation with an African-American. They talked about some technical issues concerning some problems with the banking system. He felt that his input was appreciated. Meanwhile, both President Bush and Saddam Hussein remained as dangerous father figures for him. Since he experienced conflicts around their images, we could speak about his lingering fears that "bad" fathers were still around. I noted that while on the couch, he was free to address his mental images of these leaders and tell them whatever came to his mind.

Because of Hamilton's progress toward joining a man's world and working through his Oedipal problems, he was able to help his younger son, the son who was still a child when his mother became ill and died. He still lived in another state where he was studying to become a veterinarian. During a memorable visit to him there, his son told his father about his difficult childhood, his losing his mother and feeling alone without his father's affection. In turn, Hamilton apologized and told his son how his own childhood was, and how his own mental problems prohibited him from being a better father. The father and son understood each other and they "bonded."

After "joining the men's world," Hamilton thought that he could stop his analysis and seriously asked me when we could terminate our work together. I thought about his question and the following came to my mind: Hamilton, for almost five decades, had suffered from his childhood traumas, all the time struggling to find solutions for them through keeping an unintegrated personality organization and through rituals and symptoms. In his analysis, he had done a great deal of work to change his internal structure and give up his need for rituals and symptoms that helped him avoid anxiety. He was now working through Oedipal struggles and becoming "a man" in his own right. But terminating his analysis at this time would be premature. I thought that he needed to review his changes, do more work crystallizing his "adult self," and have more life experiences with this new integrated (gray) self before we could finish our work together. I did not want to tell him all the things that came to mind. I thought it would be an intellectual response to his "playing" manhood. It would have been, I think, all right in the long run if I had shared my thoughts with him. But, in any case, I only said, "What is our hurry!" He smiled and stopped asking for a termination date for his psychoanalysis. He returned to President Bush and Saddam Hussein. He read about Saddam's upbringing and found a connection between the Iraqi leader's upbringing and his murderous acts. He was identifying with me in "psychoanalyzing" Saddam. He continued to perceive President Bush as the "whipping father" of his childhood, who said to Iraqis, "I'll whip your ass. It is for your own good. My whipping you and killing you hurts me more than it hurts you!" At the same time, Hamilton was becoming more and more involved in civic affairs in Richmond. He continually asked, "What is my role in life?" "How can I balance my own pleasures with doing good things in the community?" He became seriously involved in the arts. He was also still trying to suggest new ideas to the people in the banking field concerning certain financial issues.

Hamilton became very concerned with the increased talk about actual war in Iraq and the country's need for more able persons to fight. His concern was for his younger son, who might be called to the Marines and sent to Kuwait. This did not materialize, but his concern made Hamilton fly to visit his son again. He told his son about his analysis and how he thought he would terminate it soon. Interestingly enough, his son, without knowing what I had told Hamilton, repeated my phrase. He said, "Do not hurry, father!" His son also told Hamilton more about his childhood memories of his dying mother. One day the boy was in his terminally ill mother's bedroom when she screamed, "Get him (her son) out of here!" The boy felt rejected and devastated. Now Hamilton told his son about Della's kind nature, her suffering, and his son's distortion of the meaning of his mother's screaming. Rather than rejecting her son, she was simply in physical and mental pain and she did not want her son to see her suffering. Hamilton told his son how much his mother loved him.

Hamilton and his son felt very sad and cried together. Hamilton felt that his son was touched. He took the young man to dinner where his son told his father about his inner loneliness. The young man had a girlfriend, but still felt isolated from other people. Hearing this, Hamilton felt badly. He recognized in his son some of his own problems. He explained to his son that it was childhood trauma—the young man's experience of "love and abandonment"—that led him to feel an inner loneliness. His "bonding" to his son was crystallized. Hamilton encouraged him to go into analysis. His son did not want money from his father; he felt that if he received financial support from Hamilton, he would feel "controlled" by him. They spoke about it openly and his son, in the end, agreed to accept financial help—at least for a short time—from his father. Soon Hamilton's son entered his own analysis.

Recounting his talk with his son led Hamilton to tell me more details about Della's illness and death. He realized that he was panic-stricken when confronted with an important separation. Instead of staying by his wife, he "escaped" from home and had sex with a married woman who, not long before, had come to work in his company. When his wife's condition became worse, he impulsively fired the married woman. First, on the couch, he expressed his remorse about making love to the woman and then mistreating her by firing her. Slowly, he now understood, with my help, that by his action he was reversing roles. He was the one who loved someone first and then rejected this person. He was filled with sadness about losing his first wife and, with tears in his eyes, acknowledged having guilty feelings for not treating her better. At this time, it was the twentieth anniversary of Della's death. Now, two years after burying her ashes, he experienced guilt, remorse, and then mourning. In spite of the pain that he experienced on the couch, he knew that going through the mourning process was an adult thing to do. It was a very moving experience for me to observe—a person having so much pain for past behavior and a past lost that, because of it, he increased his own self-esteem and entered into a "man's world."

FOWLER: Hamilton continues to play as he dares to join the man's world. He is at the same time being a man and father to his son. His relationships are maturing. He returns to remorse of the losses of his wife, Della.

VOLKAN: This is an important development. He can experience remorse. Furthermore, through his further identification with the analyst and his analyzing functions, Hamilton develops further ability to analyze himself and, as we see, help his son with his mental problems. His mourning over losing Della, and his remorse for not treating her better when she was alive, point to his developing psyche. But, we had more work to do.

Chapter 10
You Have Your Tools and I Have Mine

As Christmas approached, at the beginning of the fifth year of his analysis, Hamilton remembered his "pineapple upside-down cake" which he wanted to give me a year earlier and which was left in the trunk of his car until it spoiled and smelled. He chuckled about this. He informed me that this Christmas he made no effort to bring me a gift. Instead, he developed a peculiar interest in my buttocks.

For decades I had the habit of keeping my office door open before my analysands arrived for their sessions. They would come in on time and close the door behind them before going to the couch. When they arrived in my office they would usually find me sitting in my comfortable chair behind the couch waiting for them. My analysands and I would make no social chitchat, not even to say "Hi" or "How are you?" or "I am well, thank you, and how are you?" In fact, almost all my analysands would not speak at all until taking their place on the couch. Hamilton too, from the beginning of our work together, had followed the same routine.

When he came into my office the day after recalling his pineapple upside-down cake, I was standing by my desk replacing some papers. As soon as I saw him I moved to my chair, but in doing so, for a few seconds I turned my back to him. When he lay on the couch, he informed me that while my back was turned toward him he looked at my buttocks and wondered if I had tight or loose muscles. He said that the year before, when he left the pineapple upside-down cake in his car instead of bringing it to me, we were concerned with his symbolic bowel movement. He had wondered if I would approve of his bodily product. By delaying and then not giving me the cake, he had tested himself to see if he could rebel against Dolly's/analyst's "orders." This time, Hamilton said, he was noticing my buttocks and wondering how I move my bowels. I responded by saying, "Let your mind wander." He then informed me that Mary had recently seen a physician and received a certificate from him indicating that she had developed some neurological disorder that indicated she could have difficulty driving a car. Hamilton and his lawyer believed that with the help of this "crook" physician Mary would use her "disability" to squeeze more money from the divorce. A court decision on a financial settlement was approaching. I told Hamilton that the court would give him orders as to what he must do and how much feces/money to produce. I added that this situation of the external world echoed in his internal world. I told him, "By becoming interested in my buttocks and my muscles, you are projecting yourself into me. You want me to perform your work for you, hopefully in a less conflicted way. If I do it in a less conflicted way, you can perhaps learn from me how to be realistic about what to produce and how to produce it." Then I continued: "If moving one's bowels will not satisfy the court, you want my buttocks to be whipped instead of yours. But, you see, what is in your mind, your concerns, belong to you and not to me." I reminded Hamilton that recently he had been busy developing his own adult autonomy, joining in a "men's world." I said that I hoped the purpose of his interest in my buttocks was mainly to identify with someone who is autonomous in deciding how to shit and what to shit.

The next day Hamilton opened his session with a dream:

> I was walking on a road, which was made of plastic. As I walked I kept looking behind to see how long this plastic road was.

The day's residue of this dream was drawn from a trip to the bank the day before when he used his plastic credit card to withdraw money. He told me that while he was doing this he wondered how much money he could get with his plastic card if he were forced to transfer a huge amount of funds to Mary's bank account. I told Hamilton that in his dream the plastic road behind him represented his feces/money. And once more I reminded him that the upcoming court decision stimulated "memories" of his childhood and his conflict over whether the way he defecated would please or not please Dolly and/or his mother.

Soon Hamilton reported that a financial settlement had taken place. Hamilton was ordered to pay a little over a million dollars to Mary. While this amount of money appeared to be a huge sum, he was very pleased. He expected to be ordered to pay more. Besides, the judge decided that he would pay this amount only once, with no monthly alimony payments required. I could see the relief on his face. Hamilton also informed me that his previous internal pressure to buy Christmas gifts for many women was also a thing of the past. Another of his symptoms had disappeared. He repeated on the couch that most likely it was some kind of guilt that had compelled him to "pay" these women. When I urged him to think more about what this guilt was about, he answered, "Guilt due to my incestuous feelings!"

Speaking about gifts led Hamilton to tell me that, unbeknownst to me, he managed to receive a "gift" from me and keep this knowledge a secret. He recalled how he had given me his "little boy smile" when we first met and how, because of this, he manipulated me into not charging him more for his sessions. In his mind, he had made me a "gift giver." When I heard this, I recalled that indeed I had sensed his little boy appeal when we first met. I wondered to myself if I would have asked for more money from a rich man like him if I had not noticed the little boy behind his English lord appearance. I assured myself that I would not have charged him more. Then I told Hamilton that when we started working together, I did not wish to make him "special." I did not want anything to interfere with my analytic perspective. I told him that he had made himself "special" by believing secretly that he manipulated me by his little boy smile. "You put us together in a picture and hung it on a wall in this office, symbolically speaking. It took you some years to know that it was not you with your mother in the picture hanging in your parents' bedroom; it was your dead sister Julia who was 'special.' I am glad that your secret about us is also now out in the open."

Hamilton then explained to me that all these years while we were working, deep down he maintained a suspicion that I was not giving him my "best treatment." If he manipulated me into charging him less money than I normally would, in his mind I would not do my professional best for him. I explained that by giving "gifts," he tried to deny rejections and separations and buy "love." I added that "love" bought through such a method was always a "fake love." I told him that if he had the illusion that I was a "gift giver" in the same manner as he was, then it would make sense for him to assume that our analytic work was also fake.

I explained to Hamilton that he had kept this secret in the service of protecting himself from being truly loved and then abandoned. If I only gave him fake love, then my abandonment would not be so painful. His secret was a resistance to committing himself totally to the analysis. I reminded him how he recently asked about ending our analytic work together. I suggested that it was now time for us to look at this piece of resistance so he could truly decide to accept all he had accomplished from analysis before separating from me. Otherwise, the ending of the analysis would also be a fake one.

My remarks made Hamilton very thoughtful and for the next two sessions he examined his feelings about my integrity. Then he reported with relief that he was ready to accept that I never gave him "fake love," but also that I never made him "special." If he were my special patient, he added, this would be such a burden for him. After coming to this conclusion, Hamilton was ready to tell me a second meaning concerning his interest in my buttocks. It was related to his homosexual love for me.

He related a dream in which he was following me in a crowded street, his eyes fixed on my buttocks. As long as he could see my buttocks, he would not get lost, as he made his way to the end of the crowded street, which was a building site. The idea in the dream was to build a beautiful house on this spot. I opened a toolbox and showed him my "tools," like hammers, wrenches, and nails. He admired my "tools." He wanted to start working and asked to use them, but then he realized that he had his own toolbox with him. He opened his toolbox and showed his tools to me. In the dream he knew that his "tools" were as good as mine.

When he finished reporting the dream, Hamilton said, "There is no need for you to interpret my dream. I know what it means—you are a man and I am a man." I stayed silent and he began to laugh. He told me that his asking me not to interpret his dream was itself an indication that he had his own "tools" (mind/penis) and that he could use them instead of depending on mine. Soon after this, his interest in my buttocks disappeared.

Hamilton's dream also reflected his recent purchase of an old building not far from Richmond. His aim was to renovate and repair this building and turn it into a fancy guesthouse. I thought that, business aside, buying this rundown building at this time and attempting to turn it into a functional and beautiful place had a great deal to do with his identification with a "good" Oedipal father/analyst (his following me in the dream to a building site and with my function as an analyst (repairing). Hamilton, in his transference relationship with me, had gone through what a "normal" child would, what psychoanalysts call a "homosexual position" on his way to resolving his Oedipus complex (owning his own tools).

Hamilton told me that it would take many months to turn his new property into a functional place. He imagined asking his new and prestigious African-American friend to join him during the opening ceremony for this fancy guesthouse. Around this time, "by accident" Hamilton came across a diary he had kept while still married to Mary. He told me that he looked at what he had written and concluded that Mary was right to call him "crazy." There was, he added, "evidence" of his past craziness in his diary. His notes apparently referred to his inner loneliness, depression and paranoia. He gave no details and I thought that I did not need to inquire about things, which both of us already knew.

Finding his diary was an obvious starting point for Hamilton's "second look" activities (Novey, 1968). Many analysands, after resolving their internal conflicts, "visit" their past to see how it was in reality. For example, an analysand may take a trip to a location where he passed his childhood to check the physical reality and compare it with the psychic reality of the same location. An analysand of mine, not unlike Hamilton, had a great deal of separation anxiety. One of his first memories of life was being in a creek and raising his arms to be pulled out of the water by his mother who stood on the bank. His memory was accompanied by great anxiety. Before he finished his analysis, he took a trip and actually found the location of the creek wherein he had fallen—or at least in his mind he had fallen. The creek was about five feet across and the water in it was shallow. As an adult, it was not at all scary, but for a child it was a horrifying place where he could be swept away from his mother. Hamilton's diary led him to look for other items to re-examine from his past. In various places there were many stored trunks filled with old pictures, letters, and documents, which he began looking at to learn about his and his ancestors' lives.

As Hamilton was actively involved in these "second look" activities, the Gulf War was quickly approaching. There was a "paranoid" atmosphere in American society that influenced everyone. At this time, I even met "normal" friends in Charlottesville who believed that Saddam Hussein's air force might bomb Charlottesville! When Hamilton spoke of Saddam, President Bush or others, he was able to separate his actual fears from his internal fears. I just listened to him.

President Bush had given Saddam Hussein a deadline to remove his forces from Kuwait or else. As the deadline approached, Hamilton continued to make anti-war remarks. He wished that all the money used for waging wars could be used for medical research. We recalled that Della had died from medical complications. Hamilton had gone to a social event with a beautiful woman, but he did not ask her to sleep with him. He reported that going out with this woman induced a kind of "guilt" in him, as if he were cheating on Lisa who was his regular girl friend at this time. But he was not in love with Lisa. Lisa was not idealized. There was no promise or intention from him or Lisa to spend a lifetime together. His "guilt" led Hamilton to speak of his fear of Saddam, and like my "normal" friends who had spoken of their imagination of Iraqi forces attacking Charlottesville, he briefly referred to how Iraqis might bomb Richmond. But quickly he related his thinking to his "guilt" and wish for "punishment," and worked through his conflict without my interference. He said that he wanted to tell me something that I might not like to hear since I was Turkish. He knew that Turks were fighting with a Kurdish group in Turkey and therefore, he thought I might not have empathy for Kurds in Iraq who were treated badly by Saddam Hussein. He added that he had empathy for the Kurds. Because the important thing was that he was free to speak his mind, I decided to tell him the truth about myself so that he would not develop unnecessary fantasies about me. I simply answered, "So do I."

FOWLER: Hamilton expresses empathy for the downtrodden and tortured Iraqi Kurds, and finds a link between the Kurds in Turkey and Turks and wonders if you are more or less in agreement with his position. He then wonders what you think, and you reply, "So do I." Up to this point, you have not disclosed opinions about the external world. Can you say why you decided to disclose this information at this point?

VOLKAN: At this time of his analysis Hamilton was actively redoing his Oedipal passage. During this time he compares me, as a new Oedipal father object with many images of his original father of his childhood. If I were like Saddam and tortured and killed the Kurds I could not be a benign Oedipal father figure. Since I am a Turkish-American and since there is a Kurdish problem in Turkey, I sensed that he was anxious about going against me if I were against the Kurds. I felt that my telling him about my empathy for the Kurds would be, in a sense, a correction of his transference distortion. However, I did not go into details of the Kurdish issue in Turkey at that time.

FOWLER: I wonder if there are times when the analysand is functioning at a different psychological level, where a disclosure of this sort is less problematic or even warranted?

VOLKAN: When a patient makes a statement about the analyst and it is true, the analyst should be careful not to disturb the analysand's correct reality testing. This does not mean to create a situation in that the analyst and the analysand become involved in spending time getting to know one another's internal worlds. The analysand should not be put in a position to "cure" the analyst. As it is recalled I had "allowed" him to see me like Saddam or Hitler without interference at earlier times. Here too, I might let him see me as a harsh Kurd hater for a while. But, I sensed that he wanted me to remain as a benign father figure in order to continue working on his resolution of the Oedipus complex. I do not know other reasons of my allying myself with him at this time.

Meanwhile, his "second look" activities led him to find pictures of his father dressing up like a famous clown. Hamilton recalled how, when his own children were small, they would visit his parents' house, especially on Sundays. His father then would put on his clown costume and entertain his grandchildren. As he told me about this, tears came to Hamilton's eyes. This image of his father was not like his perception of Saddam Hussein or President Bush. Hamilton wished that his father had been nice to him too, when he was a child, instead of taking him to the "torture chamber." Recalling his father's "niceness" toward his grandchildren, Hamilton spoke of breaking the "bad" generational link. Now his grandchildren were happy. They knew nothing about a "torture chamber." Hamilton, however, did not wish his grandchildren to be exposed to fears about a war. The approaching Gulf War also led him to investigate another war: the American Civil War, and its influence on his ancestors and, in turn, on himself.

Chapter 11
The Gulf War and the Mannequins of the American Civil War

Hamilton arrived at his January 17, 1991, session uncharacteristically ten minutes late. While waiting for him, I felt concerned, wondering what might have happened to him. Was he in an accident? When he arrived I kept my thoughts to myself and he spoke first. He reported that he had stayed up very late the night before watching the beginning of the Gulf War on television—a devastating air assault against targets in Iraq and Kuwait. He said that it was like watching a sports event, a football or basketball game. This angered him since he knew that people were being killed and families ruined. He reported a sense of isolation and loneliness while watching the air assault on television and he knew that these were feelings from his childhood. "I slept late and I did not wake up to come to my session on time," he added and did not apologize. I sensed that, in view of the war and all its horrors, an apology for being ten minutes late for the luxury of being analyzed would be out of place. Also, our getting together was not a social event that warranted such niceties. I thought that by being late he made me the isolated and lonely, as well as angry, child for ten minutes. I knew then why I had uncomfortable feelings while I was waiting for him, worried about him being in an accident. I decided not to share this with Hamilton. It appeared that he had already taken his "bad" feelings back and I thought there was no need for me to "accuse" him of projecting his uncomfortable feelings into me. After all, it was all right for me to have brief, firsthand emotional information about the depressive mood of his childhood. Furthermore, not all of those ten minutes with long and rather severe discomfort was due to my sensing Hamilton's projections, however distant he was from my office.

Wars or war-like situations remind me of the death of my roommate when I was a medical student at the University of Ankara in Turkey in the 1950s. His name was Erol and he was like my younger brother. In 1957 I came to the United States as a newly graduated medical doctor. A few months later, Erol went to Cyprus to visit his ailing mother. Cypriot Greek EOKA (Ethniki Organosis Kyprion Agoniston) terrorists were trying to drive the governing British out in order to unite the island with Greece. (For details see: Volkan, 1979.) They were also terrorizing the island's Turks who opposed the unification. When Erol went to a pharmacy to buy some medicine for his mother, EOKA terrorists shot him seven times—simply because he was an intelligent medical student. His death shocked the Cypriot Turkish community. All this happened while I was safely in Chicago. It took me a very long time to realize that I had developed a severe case of "survival guilt." I realized it could have been me who was killed, but I survived and Erol died. Even though I worked through my survival guilt during my own training analysis (going through one's own analysis is required for someone who will be a future analyst), "memories" of my survival guilt had remained, and watching the beginning of the Gulf War on television—like Hamilton did the night before—was not like watching a sterile television war game for me either. I kept my feelings and thoughts to myself while Hamilton was on my couch.

The night after our session, Hamilton had a vague dream about Saddam Hussein in which he sensed that Saddam was dangerous. The next day he found himself calling Mary "for some legal business," although his lawyer had been dealing with her and Hamilton was not internally preoccupied with her. He knew that he was doing something unusual. On the phone, Mary was nasty to him. When Hamilton told me about his Saddam dream and his calling Mary, I suggested that as a child he might perceive his mother's (Mary's) punishing him to be more tolerable than his father's (Saddam Hussein's) punishing him. He agreed.

Hamilton reported that he was hesitant to tell me about his calling Mary. He thought that I might "whip" him. His old symptom of creating a dangerous father in others had returned, at least temporarily, mainly because of his watching the war on television. He had seen prisoners of war displayed on the screen, and he told me how such scenes induced his recollection of his own shame and helplessness as a child. He was experiencing an opportunity to have a "second look" at his childhood. He recalled how he used to think of me as a "Terrible Turk" with a scimitar. He said that it amused him to realize that my scary image was very mild in comparison to his present image of President Bush with an IBM missile performing "surgical strikes."

That night while the air assaults against targets in Iraq and Kuwait were still going on, Hamilton went to a fancy dinner party. As he informed me the next day, he was seated next to a rich lady from Iran who, Hamilton sensed, was also in turmoil over the war. She had escaped the oppressive regime in Iran, but nevertheless she wanted to boast about her country and narcissistically defend herself against aggressive Americans, even though she did not like the Iraqis who had fought against the Iranians. According to Hamilton, at one point the Iranian woman declared that six-year-old Iranian children were better educated than twelve-year-old American youngsters. She added that in Iran children behave better than American children because Iranian parents whip their children if they misbehave. Hamilton felt that this Iranian woman jumped on him. "I wasn't going to take it." He added, "I wanted to misbehave and be sure that I was not whipped." Hamilton described how, by raising his voice for others to hear, he told the Iranian woman that whipping children was a form of child abuse. Then he said to her, "I want you to know that American children are as educated as Iranian children and little girls in America are not forced to wear veils." Apparently people around the table watched this "battle" between Hamilton and the Iranian woman. Hamilton, in fact, was having a "second look" at his childhood helplessness and reversing it. When he realized this, he stopped "fighting" with the Iranian lady. But that night he had a dream that Iraqi soldiers were shooting at him; bullets were coming through a three or four foot wooden board. [The reader will recall the wooden board at the end of his parents' bed that was above a smaller bed where little Hamilton slept whenever he was ill and had a fever.] In the dream, Hamilton was shot and died. He was put in a tomb, and although he was dead, he could see people around his tomb. They were all dressed up. His mother was there next to a woman—the Iranian woman—who was wearing a beautiful fur coat. Then a strange thing happened. He had a "rebirth." He got out of his tomb and began walking around. All the people began to become like mannequins, some of them African-Americans. He wanted to put these mannequins into the tomb that he had just vacated.

Hamilton thought that his interaction with the Iranian woman had taken him back to his childhood and the mannequins were important figures of his childhood and his ancestors. He felt that he was "reborn" as an adult, and now he could look at these figures, understand their influence on him, and then turn them into mannequins and bury them (repress them).

Hamilton was aware that, more than his encounter with the Iranian woman, his watching the air assaults on television created his urgency to look at the important people in his past, even people he never met because he was born after they had died. First, he began telling me about the American Civil War. I was like his pupil. "Do you know how many lives were destroyed or disturbed during the Civil War?" he would ask and then would add, "Disease during the Civil War killed twice as many people as bullets and bayonets did. Wait and see. After this Gulf War, civilians in Iraq will suffer." No one in Hamilton's family was killed during the American Civil War except a great-uncle who was only eighteen years old when he died. But, Hamilton, on the couch, kept counting how many scars the American Civil War left on his family. The Civil War was certainly present in Dolly's mind, and he recalled a trunk in Dolly's house filled with Civil War pictures. As a child, stories about these pictures were told and retold in the family.

Now more than ever Hamilton realized that, besides the influence of actual childhood experiences in the development of his personality organization rituals and his symptoms, what passed from generation to generation also played a key role in who he would become.

Hamilton began to examine the ghosts awakened by the Gulf War and piece together his ancestors' story. The reader, like myself, will notice that Hamilton was already aware of some pieces of his ancestors' story.

FOWLER: Perhaps at this point we should pause and take a closer look at the idea of passing psychological elements from generation to generation, and especially the concept of generational transmission of trauma.

VOLKAN: Passing psychological elements especially the influence of a trauma to next generation(s) owes a great deal to studies made of the second and third generations of Holocaust survivors and others directly traumatized under the Third Reich (references to many studies on this topic can be found in Kogan,

1998, Kestenberg and Brenner, 1996; Volkan, Ast, and Greer, 2002). Psychoanalytic clinical work and research (too many to list here) shows that there is fluidity between a child's "psychic borders" and those of the mother and other caretakers. The child-mother/caretaker experiences generally function as a kind of "incubator" for the child's developing mind. Besides growth-initiating elements, however, the caretaker from the older generation can also transmit undesirable psychological elements to the child. One of the best-known examples of a relatively simple negative form of transgenerational transmission comes from Anna Freud and Dorothy Burlingham's (1943) observations of women and children during the Nazi attacks on London. Freud and Burlingham noted that infants under three did not become anxious during the bombings unless their mothers were afraid. The fluidity mentioned above also occurs in drastic ways among adults under certain conditions of regression, such as during and after massive catastrophes at the hand of others.

There are many forms of transgenerational transmission. Besides anxiety, depression, elation, or worries, there are various psychological tasks that one person may "assign" to another. The well-known phenomenon of the "replacement child" (Cain and Cain, 1964; Poznanski, 1972) illustrates the transmission of psychological tasks. A child dies; soon after, the mother becomes pregnant again, and the second child lives. The mother "deposits" (Volkan, 1987) her image of the dead child—including her affective relationship with the dead child—into the developing identity of her second child. The second child now has the task of keeping this "deposited" identity within him or herself, and there are different ways for the child to respond to this task. The child may adapt to being a replacement child by successfully "absorbing" what has been deposited. Alternately, the child may develop a "double identity," experiencing what we call a "borderline personality organization." Or, the second child may be doomed to try to live up to the idealized image of the dead sibling within, becoming obsessively driven to excel. Similarly, adults who are drastically traumatized may deposit their traumatized self-images into the developing identities of their children. A Holocaust survivor who appears well adjusted may be able to behave "normally" because he has deposited aspects of his traumatized self-images into his children's developing selves and has given the children "tasks" to deal with these images (Brenner, 1999). His children, then, are the ones now responding to the horror of the Holocaust, "freeing" the older victim from his burden. As with replacement children, such children's own responses to being carriers of injured parental self-images vary because of each child's individual psychological make-up that is independent of the deposited images and the child's specific external conditions.

The air assault on targets in Iraq and Kuwait, as I said, began on January 16, 1991. The ground war began on February 24 and only lasted four days. U.S. and coalition forces entered Kuwait City on February 26. Iraqis set fire to over 500 of Kuwait's oil wells as they withdrew from Kuwait. On our television screens we watched a raging inferno. On March 3, Iraq agreed to abide by all of the

U.N. resolutions and an official cease-fire was signed on April 6. As he witnessed these events, Hamilton developed an overall picture of his ancestors' history as completely as he could. The rest of this chapter describes how this research affected his psychological development. Starting with the next chapter, I will return to this period of time in Hamilton's psychoanalysis and report other therapeutic stories.

Hamilton's paternal grandmother, Dolly, was the youngest of seven siblings. She was six years old when the South was defeated and the American Civil War ended. A few years earlier, her father had left their farm to join the war. There was no information as to whether or not their farm was raided or ruined during the war. According to Dolly's stories, the family lived in fear of hunger, rape and death. Dolly grew up in an atmosphere where her mother and her older siblings were anxious, and their previously comfortable lifestyle was gone.

White masters' relationships with Negro slaves had changed; one slave on Dolly's farm named King had worked for Dolly's father most of his life and was considered trustworthy and loyal. When Dolly's father went to war, King was already elderly or, in Dolly's mind, he was an elderly and kind man. Dolly knew that King was appointed as her "protector," although it was not clear if Dolly's father had asked King to look after his little girl before he went to war. When Hamilton was growing up, she would say, "I loved King." Even in her late years, Dolly would use many occasions to recall her childhood love companion and repeat: "I loved King."

When the Civil War ended, Dolly's traumatized father returned to his farm and family. One day soon after this, without giving notice, King escaped to the North. The family never heard from King again. Now, going over his family's history and putting pieces together, Hamilton realized that Dolly, too, was a person who was "loved and abandoned." A similar story would repeat itself in Hamilton's life when Abigail left him and he never heard from her again. Now, Hamilton thought that Dolly played a role in urging her son and daughter-in-law—Hamilton's parents—to "fire" Abigail because Dolly had never forgiven King, even though she continued to "love" him, as Hamilton continued to "love" Abigail. Dolly, Hamilton now believed, took revenge by urging Abigail's exile.

Hamilton reported that Dolly grew up fearing separations. After the Civil War, when all her siblings left the farm, Dolly stayed, feeling obligated to look after her parents. She also made dresses for her siblings and to sell for money. Her brothers and sisters eventually married. As some became professionals, like teachers or preachers, Dolly remained an "old maid." In those days, a woman was expected to marry in her late teens or twenties, but Dolly would not marry, as will be described soon, until she was thirty years old.

After the Civil War, one of Dolly's brothers went to Germany and studied medicine, although Hamilton had no idea why his great uncle chose to go to Germany. When he returned, he joined the family on the farm and practiced medicine in the community. Dolly had many memories of her doctor brother and would talk about him as Hamilton was growing up. Hamilton realized that it was this great uncle who originally had come across the writings of a "German doctor," and he now also knew the name of this "German doctor": Daniel Gottlob Moritz Schreber, who died in 1861, the year the American Civil War began. Apparently, Dr. Schreber's image as a "great figure" remained in Hamilton's great uncle's mind and, as we will see, he acted accordingly. When Hamilton asked me what I knew about Dr. Schreber, I decided to tell him that indeed, others also thought of him as a giant of his day. I informed Hamilton that when Dr. Schreber died, another physician gave a eulogy and spoke of Dr. Schreber as a "giant."

Hamilton reported that Dolly's doctor brother might have been an angry man, also traumatized by the American Civil War and the loss of the family fortune. When he returned to the United States, he made his then unmarried sister his "nigger." At the time, Dolly was still taking care of her parents. Now, she began to take care of her doctor brother. Hamilton believed that this German educated brother put Dr. Schreber's ideas into practice in dealing with his youngest sister. Hamilton recalled Dolly's memories of how her brother treated her. He would say, "Nigger, bring me water!" "Nigger, bring me a chair." It appeared to us that by having his sister as a "nigger," this man re-created the pre-Civil War family, which had slaves. Dolly later would say that she "willingly" became her brother's slave.

Hamilton and I wondered why Dolly masochistically submitted to her brother. By the time I was introduced to Dolly she was already dead. She had never been on my couch. But I thought that making some sense of Dolly's behavior would help Hamilton. Thus, I joined Hamilton in speculating about Dolly's behavior. Perhaps by becoming a "nigger" and blindly serving a "master" (her brother), she was creating in reverse fashion her own "secure" life with King. Assuming Dr. Schreber's method of childrearing, and obviously modifying it to respond to his own internal wishes and fears, her brother was shutting down the emotions of the scared, Civil War era child within Dolly, and in turn denying his own possible traumas.

Dolly saved herself from being her brother's "nigger" when she married at age thirty, and Hamilton also had a story to tell about this marriage. He assumed that Dolly was a person who, deep down, felt hurt and humiliated. Apparently it was important for her to be married before she was thirty, because if a woman was thirty and not married, she was really an "old maid." Her husband was some months younger than Dolly, therefore when she married, she lied and told others that she was twenty-nine and the man she married was twenty-nine-and-a-half. When Hamilton told this story, he and I wondered if Hamilton's search for a woman in her thirties might also have something to do with his grandmother's refusing to be known as a thirty-year-old bride. Did Hamilton, who was mistreated by Dolly, want to unmask his grandmother's secret by finding a woman who was already in her thirties? We would never know the answer to this question, but the question itself came to our mind. There was also another unanswered question. Did Hamilton attempt to find a kind of freedom from Dolly by insisting that his idealized woman should be in her thirties since Dolly, the oppressor, would not admit to being thirty years old when she got married?

Dolly's husband, who died when Hamilton was five years old, was known as a person who had very mild manners. Adult Hamilton knew—he had heard from others while growing up—that Dolly had dominated her husband's life, making him her "slave," as her brother had made her his "slave." It appeared that married Dolly had identified with her brother and his image of Dr. Schreber.

When her husband died, Dolly moved to the home of her daughter, Hamilton's aunt, and soon "adopted" a black boy who became her shadow. When Dolly came to Hamilton's house, especially on Sundays, she usually would not bring the black boy with her. If he came along, he would stay outside of the main house. Dolly would also say that she "loved" this black boy. It occurred to Hamilton and me that Dolly had to repeat her childhood trauma and create a "Dolly-King" pair again and again, perhaps until she died. We also assumed that the little black boy at some level symbolically stood for King who would now be under Dolly's absolute control. He would not leave her. It was clear that, at least to some extent, Hamilton "learned" this method of controlling a love companion from Dolly.

During her visits to Hamilton's house, as I wrote earlier, Dolly would speak of hungry children around the globe (who most likely represented her "hungry" child self), and she would constantly talk about the American Civil War. Of course, she would also recommend that her son's children, the boys, be whipped until they stopped crying. This would be good for building character. Hamilton now understood how humiliated and angry Dolly was and how she projected her own "hungry" childhood images from the Civil War days onto her grandchildren and how she took revenge on King's leaving her by bringing Dr. Schreber into Hamilton's household.

Hamilton also recalled how Dolly disciplined her own children. While her husband never hit the children, Dolly disciplined them. Hamilton remembered a story that he had heard from his father. As a child, Hamilton's father left a pair of shoes in the yard against his mother's orders. She put him out and locked the door to the house, making the child (Hamilton's father) stay out in the cold all night. She told him that this hurt her more than it hurt Hamilton's father, but she did it to build up his character. Hamilton knew that his father, identifying with his own mother, who had identified with her brother/Dr. Schreber, used the same tactics to build character in his sons.

We wondered why Hamilton's mother went along with her mother-in-law's rules in raising her children. Hamilton collected data about her maternal grandmother by talking to his older siblings, and learned that his maternal grandmother's family was also traumatized during the American Civil War. His maternal grandmother, Hamilton was told, was a "perfectionist" and her daughter, Hamilton's mother, was very dependent on her and always sought her approval. Hamilton now thought that when his mother lost her first child, Julia, she might have felt she was no longer a "perfect daughter" for her mother. At the time Hamilton's mother became depressed when he was three years old, her mother had died and she had moved from the location where Julia and her mother were buried. I joined Hamilton in speculating that his mother used Dolly as an external punitive agent (psychoanalytically speaking, as a punitive superego), which permitted direct expression of her anger, as when beating her sons, and thus gave her temporary relief from turning her aggression towards herself (her depression).

After examining the "mannequins" in his dream, Hamilton was ready to bury them in "the grave" he had vacated.

FOWLER: Could you comment on the process of Hamilton reviewing his family? It seems that the intensity of the transference to you is less hot now as he learns new things about his family, integrating them into his therapeutic story.

VOLKAN: Hamilton is reviewing his gains, and "taking stock" at this phase of analysis is another important issue (I will say more about this in the next chapter). He had thought he was getting ready to finish his analysis. But then an external war became intertwined with his internal wars. This gave him an opportunity to examine what was passed to him from his ancestors. The transference still is there. But it is to a "new object." I am his companion investigating the importance of transgenerational transmission in his life. We are two men working together. Throughout his life, Hamilton sometimes experienced his parents and Dolly as monsters, as Nazis, and kept such "bad" images split and away from defensively idealized "good" images that he constantly tried to collect. During his analysis he was able to mend his opposite object (others') images and corresponding image of himself. Now by looking at the history of his ancestors he sees Dolly and his parents as people caught up in a traumatizing environment with their corresponding internal problems. They shrink from being monsters to people with their own problems. What is far more important is the patient's grasp of the role of transgenerational transmissions in his own psychopathology. Then Hamilton is able to let go of the ghosts from his past. In a sense he says, "They don't belong to me. I can let them go." After examining the "mannequins" in his dream, Hamilton was ready to bury them for good in "the tomb" he had created.

During this time, Hamilton and I took an extra step, and brought the ancestors' drama and its influence on Hamilton to his analysis, and I believe that this allowed Hamilton to have a more comprehensive analysis. In turn, as we will see in the next chapter, he became interested in his grandchildren even more and wanted to break any influence of their ancestors' problems starting with the American Civil War. Would Hamilton have successfully finished his analysis had he not examined his internal intertwining of his ancestors' reactions to historical events with his own personal traumas during his developmental years? Perhaps the answer is, "yes." But his understanding of himself as a "reservoir" of the mental images of individuals who were humiliated and hurt by a war and left with masochistic and sadistic character traits, I believe, allowed Hamilton to obtain a better internal freedom in dealing with himself and his environment.

The controversy about bringing the danger, resulting from wars, war-like conditions, and drastic political change into the psychoanalytic process still continues. I am in favor of paying attention to such changes in the external world and acute or chronic historical crises that may enter our physical environments. Furthermore, I tried to illustrate how the mental representation of our ancestors' historical events sometimes plays a crucial role in our psychological make-up. I am suggesting that the analyst should take into consideration the various types of transgenerational transmissions. I also wish to repeat that paying attention to history should only be done in a way that illustrates how past actual trauma, war, war-like conditions, and drastic political changes—their mental representations—intertwine with our internal developmental issues, wishes, defenses, conflicts, and fantasies. When, within the analytic setting, our analysands experience that some of their symptoms or personality traits originally belonged to their ancestors or were initiated by past historical events, they have a better chance of freeing themselves from the troubling influences of such symptoms or character traits. They will also have a better chance of working through the transference manifestations associated with ancestors and people who lived before their birth when they face wars, war-like conditions or drastic political change.

Chapter 12
Taking Stock

While the most devastating air assaults in history were taking place against Iraqi targets, one day Hamilton bought a new pair of shoes. That night he had a dream that his new shoes did not fit his feet—they were the wrong size, too small for his feet. On the couch he asked me what his dream meant. I told him to reverse his statement describing his dream. He said, "My feet are too large for the pair of shoes," and then added, "I have grown up." His mind went to his childhood loneliness. This time he became aware that his father knew that his son felt alone. He remembered that when he was a child during the Great Depression, his father had to leave the house early in the morning to supervise the work on the farm, but before he left, he would often assure little Hamilton that he would be back for lunch. Before departing, Hamilton's "papa" would suggest a method to deal with loneliness. He would tell his son "to count" while waiting, in order not to feel lonely. On the couch Hamilton reported that his father would tell him to figure out how long it would take to run from one end of a particular field to the other end. Or, the little boy was asked to count in his mind how many bales of hay were needed to complete loading a particular wagon. After that, the boy could figure out how many men would be required to carry out this or that task on the farm.

I told Hamilton that following his father's suggestions might have played a role in his becoming a successful industrialist and businessman. His father's "methodology" taught him to imagine tasks and how to calculate finishing them. But, I added, his father also contributed to the development of his rituals (his obsessionalism) to deal with his bad feelings. "The counting various things in order to manage your childhood loneliness was a ritual and this method was handed down to you by your father." Soon this type of interaction appeared in his transference relationship with me. Hamilton said that since he was now a grown-up person, I should give him a "command" and say, "You are cured! You can leave your analytic work now and walk away." I asked him to wonder why he needed "my command." He realized that he wanted me, like the father of his childhood, to suggest a method for dealing with a psychological task. This time the task was his separation from me. Besides, Hamilton realized, my giving him a "command" would make me a "German" since, in his mind, Germans have a habit of giving orders to their children. I told him that he might be speaking only about one German: Dr. Schreber who lived on in his grandmother Dolly's mind. This exchange between us led me to discuss with Hamilton the idea of "mutuality." "Can you imagine," I asked him, "deciding together to reach a termination date for our work? Can you imagine the separation between us as different than the devastating separations of your childhood?" I added, "Can you also imagine that the separation between us would not be traumatic, but enriching?"

The next day he watched some prisoners-of-war on television and reported on the couch that it was ridiculous to talk about such prisoners in a civilized manner as the television commentator had done. He was also referring to me, I thought. I was telling him about "mutuality" in a civilized and intellectual manner while he still felt his childhood loneliness. Loneliness was also represented by the conditions of the prisoners of war, and when he saw them, he thought about a separation between us. What I thought was correct. Hamilton wanted to "bargain" with me further about how we would end his analysis. He still searched for a "command" or suggestions from me for "rituals." When I did not respond, he started his next session with the following statement: "I agree with you that I want to use my past patterns dealing with separations to handle terminating my analysis. But now my patterns are also different than those I used in the past." I stayed silent and he explained to me how his pattern when separating from me would be different. He said that I tolerated his neurosis so long and that even his telling me mean things (about me and others) became easier for him because he trusted me for not retaliating against him. When the time came to separate from me he could speak his mind freely and if the separation angered him he could report that, too.

Hamilton then spoke of how it would still be easier for him if he followed an order given by me. After all, he added, he had gotten dependent on me; I played the role of his family members in his mind and now he perceived me as a substitute, guiding father. I told him that his perceptions were correct, but he had gone through such experiences with me in the service of gaining his own autonomy in the long run.

The next day Hamilton began taking stock of his changes, without being aware that he was doing so. I sensed that he was going to "count evidence" for me of his new way of feeling, behaving, and having his own autonomy in deciding how to live his life. I thought that this type of "counting" was also good for crystallizing his new self and his new ego functions. There was not much for me to do but sit behind the couch and listen. Here are some examples of events he "counted" to illustrate how he had behaved in "new ways."

He opened the session with excitement. I was like a male friend with whom he wanted to share something funny that had happened to him. "Oh! Oh!" he said, "I have a 'pussy pill story' to tell you." He proceeded to describe how a beautiful woman in her thirties arrived at his place of business in a fancy car wearing a silk scarf and a short skirt. She was spectacular and a divorcee. She had called Hamilton the day before saying that she wanted to meet him and to ask for his advice about a business matter. She then proceeded to tell Hamilton about what kind of advice she was seeking, and Hamilton responded that he was not an expert in the issues she was asking about. Nevertheless, the next day without an invitation, she appeared at Hamilton's office.

Hamilton was laughing when he was describing this woman to me. He knew that she had heard about Hamilton's former reputation as a "lady's man" and was just looking for a good time. She was available for a love affair. Hamilton reported with some pride, "I did not take the bait!"

A second event also reminded him of his childhood and provided "evidence" about his changes. Hamilton was at a clothing store, which in reality was called "The Young Men's Shop." The name of the shop was appropriate, Hamilton said, because he was a "young man" in his own mind. At the store, he was looking at suits. A rich woman in her mid-sixties whom he knew happened to be in this store, too. She came up to Hamilton and told him that she had given money to a civic organization. She then "ordered" Hamilton to do the same. Hamilton noted that this woman reminded him of Dolly. In the past such an encounter would make him feel uncomfortable, but this time he did not feel bad or anxious and he had no intention of following this woman's "orders." But when he realized that there was also an African-American minister in the store whom he liked, Hamilton bought a forty-five dollar tie for him as a gift. The minister was appreciative of Hamilton's gesture. Later, Hamilton realized that the "child" in him had determined even his generosity. Upon reflection however, he thought this was all right and the "child" was able to determine what to do by himself. He could choose to be generous toward someone while not being generous to an organization to which he did not belong.

That night Hamilton had a dream in which he was a young man. In the dream, he had to go to a high school in town some miles away from Williamsburg. He had no transportation, but he decided that he could walk to the school, and so he began walking. Upon awakening, Hamilton analyzed his dream. His father had an employee, a black man, who was originally from this town. This black man also had no transportation to work but he would hitchhike and never hesitated walking in order to get to a place where work was available. Hamilton used to admire this man for his "independence." He said that his dream reflected his new habits and his "independence."

The next day during his session Hamilton "counted" another event that illustrated his new way of responding to things that reminded him of his childhood. The day before he had gone to the run-down diner in downtown Richmond for a sandwich. While there, the African-American co-owner of the establishment told Hamilton that she was going to be married in a few months' time, move to another city, and sell her share of the diner to her long-term partner, the African-American man. Upon hearing the news, Hamilton said, he observed the return of his childhood depression. It was like Abigail informing him of her departure. The African-American woman was a "real mamma" type, sexy and possessing a good sense of humor. She used to sing for him. Hamilton realized that he would miss her, but he also realized that his happiness would not depend on this woman staying in Richmond. His depression was lifted. But, after leaving the diner, he observed another thing that amused him. While driving back to his office, it occurred to him that he should buy insurance for catastrophic events. After all, there was trouble in the Gulf region and in the Middle East and bad things could happen in the U.S.A. too. Then he realized that the "catastrophic event" was the departure of the diner's female owner, the departure of Abigail. He was amused. He changed his mind about buying new insurance.

That night Hamilton had a dream about a brick wall from the American Civil War time. The place looked like the ruins of Pompeii he had seen in some pictures. In the dream his job was to clean the field of old bricks and pieces of glass that were strewn on the ground. He said that the brick and the glass represented the "mannequins" he had dreamed about previously.

In spite of his "taking stock" and observing how he had changed, the idea of separating from me was still making him anxious. In one dream he took off in an airplane from "mother earth," but he could not fly high enough. In another dream he saw himself as a small child wearing a bathrobe and carrying a suitcase that looked like a pillow. He was at a train station. There he saw a couple. The woman wore a brown hat like Hamilton's mother used to wear when Hamilton was a youngster and the man wore a light brown coat like one his father had worn. In the dream Hamilton sensed that the couple stood for his parents, but he felt that they were behaving as if they were strangers. He felt alone. He was supposed to choose a destination, but did not know where to go.

When associating to the dream, Hamilton spoke of recognizing that the train station was the one from where his older brother departed when he was sent to serve in the U.S. military. At that time Hamilton was still a teenager. The train station was very crowded and confusing. Hamilton's father approached a porter, gave him $5, and asked him to find a place for his son to sit during the journey. The porter succeeded in finding a seat for Hamilton's brother. Hamilton recalled how proud he was for having a father who could get things done. He spoke of his dream wish that when it was time for our separation, I would put him on a train, find a seat for him, choose his destination, and send him there. On the couch he became very sad. He was now sixty-three years old. He thought about getting old. If he were psychologically becoming a "young man" who could make decisions for himself, he would only have a limited number of years to live differently. But, nevertheless, he was willing to do so if I gave him instruction about how he should terminate his analysis.

I noticed that at this time he was speaking of a good and helpful father image, instead of referring to a bad father who would whip him in order to make him behave. But, I noticed that his wished-for identification with a good father would still be contaminated with the "memories" of a whipping father. He spoke of his first marriage and his honeymoon. At that time he had suffered from premature ejaculation. On the other hand, his wife did not know how to reach orgasm even after he "cured" his premature ejaculation by going to bed with an older woman who taught him how to prolong his erection. Hamilton felt cheated. A memory of his identification with his whipping father came to him. He and his first wife were in a hotel room in Washington, D.C., naked in bed. She could not reach orgasm and she was angry and sulking. He wanted more sex, but she was not in the mood. He slapped her. Hamilton, on the couch, reported to me how guilty he had felt then. The next day he sent her roses and never again raised his hand against her. The night after recalling this incident and reporting it to me, Hamilton had a dream of his black dog from his teenage years ejaculating. We talked about how the dog represented Hamilton who was angry at rejecting women. When he ejaculated on Dorothy's leg and tummy, he was an ejaculating dog. When he used to call me "good boy," he was transferring the ejaculating dog image onto me.

Hamilton continued to examine his expectations of what would happen to him when we terminated his analysis. During this period, his dreams referred to his leaving home for military school in Maryland and his anxieties about being away. He, as I indicated in the last chapter, also continued to examine the "mannequins" of his ancestors and keep an eye on what was happening in the Gulf region. When President Bush ordered a unilateral cease-fire on February 27, 1991, Hamilton reported learning that Americans had killed an estimated one hundred thousand Iraqis in order to claim victory. "We (Americans) have such joy." He continued, "as if the war was an athletic event and we won it." He stated: "We want to kill Saddam because he is also within ourselves." He wanted to kill Saddam within himself, he said, and added that he did not need to be joyful about it. As he continued to speak, he realized that totally getting rid of Saddam within himself and wiping out his previously unconscious fantasy of "murdering" his siblings and rejecting caregivers would mean that he would no longer need or wish for me to stay around. The termination of our work together would come and this would be like his "killing" me too. He thought about young Dolly's inability to leave her parents' home after the American Civil War. During his analysis, Hamilton said, he had gone through a war, but he did not wish to be like Dolly, stuck with traumatized (and traumatizing) parents and taking care of them. He declared that he needed courage to separate from me. But the memory of going to military school where some of his ancestors had gone, but then only tolerating the few years he stayed there, haunted him. If we terminated and separated (if he went to military school), would he be able to tolerate remaining independent?

During his psychoanalytic hours that followed, he could not get away from the topic of separation from me. He told me how his father went to a social party and afterwards died in his sleep. He wanted to be sure that if I "die" after our separation, my death would not be painful. But, in turn, he wanted me to give him "parting advice" so that he would not be homesick for my couch. Then he remembered going away to a summer camp when he was a youngster. His father told him to learn how to swim, and with the help of a young man there, he did learn how to swim. He was not anxious to return home, but when he did go back, his father was proud of his son for learning how to swim. A smile appeared on Hamilton's face when he reported this memory. I said to him, "There is hope." His smile widened.

On the couch Hamilton went back to "taking stock," which included looking more closely at the mannequins of his ancestors. He recalled in 1945 his brother was in the military and stationed in South Carolina. During a trip back home, his brother told Hamilton how he could not believe the way some white folks treated the black people in South Carolina. Hamilton recalled Dolly's dealing with blacks. Her grandchildren were forbidden to say anything humiliating to African-Americans. When blacks were ill, Dolly would nurse them to health. When blacks died, she would send flowers to their funerals. Yet, Dolly would get upset if a black servant came near the front entrance of her house without a reason. She would then shout, "Nigger, what are you doing in front of the house?" Hamilton once more put Dolly's good and bad images together. When he finished doing so, he began to speak about me. He recalled my telling him things like, "I want to shout at you" when his repetition of some of his rituals bored me. Then he recalled that whenever I told him that I was bored, I added that I knew how much more bored he was with his endless repetitions, and that he was making me feel his boredom for him. He recalled that I never punished him; I was gentle and stable, but every time my voice rose, he would remember that Turks were warriors. "Why did you sometimes shout at me?" he asked. I answered, "Because your neurosis was shouting louder and I wanted to be heard." He burst into laughter.

That night Hamilton had a dream and reported it in his next session with me. In the dream he was walking around a farm where there were cattle. Then he noticed there were little animals attached to the ground. They looked like cabbages. He thought in the dream that these little animals were like the mines left in the field in Kuwait. He began stomping on them in order to destroy them.

After reporting this dream on the couch, Hamilton recalled buying a farm, when he was a young man, like the one that appeared in his dream. The farm came with cattle. He bought it for ninety thousand dollars, a good buy. Soon he sold this farm in an auction for over two hundred thousand dollars. His father had helped him financially to buy this farm. He added that I also had helped him profit from his analysis (in reality, recently he had made a great deal of money in the stock market), but there was still some neurosis attached to his psyche (soil). He told me that he was killing the remnants of his neurosis before we set up a termination date. He described to me how cabbage roots remain in the soil if you cut off the vegetable. But if a person stomps on a cabbage, the roots are killed and the cabbage will not come back to life. In his dream, he realized, he was getting rid of the last vestiges of his neurosis.

For some days after this dream and his own interpretation of it, Hamilton was concerned with the idea of "death." He also knew that his thinking about death was connected with his preoccupation with finishing his analysis. He was still dating Lisa, but now and then was also seeing other women. He asked me, "Are you waiting for me to commit myself to only one woman before you consider me totally cured?" Then he added, "Is the idea of one woman for a man your criteria for my being well?" I told him that I had no such criteria. What we learned during our work, I added, was that he had a fantasy of "killing" his younger sisters and rejecting caretakers, but at the same time he was addicted to "pussy pills." Since his fantasy was no longer unconscious and since his addiction was gone, he would know the future course of his relationships with women.

This hour was on a Friday. When he came to his session on Monday, Hamilton told me that he had done something most unusual and for the first time over the weekend. He stayed at home alone all day Saturday and cooked an elaborate dinner for himself and made bread. He was happy while he was cooking. He said that he felt no loneliness. I told him that what he did was a response to our talk about the idea of "one woman" and his previous need for "pussy pills." He wanted to prove that within him was a caring woman who would feed him physically and emotionally. Therefore, he could now deal with women in real life according to more adult expectations.

Hamilton began to wonder out loud on the couch what he might do in the post-analytic period of his life. He spoke of running his company another seven or eight years. He also referred to us, and said that he would feel comfortable leaving me in one month, but wondered if it would be an abrupt departure. He stated, "I am thinking that my coming to your office has been like visiting somebody's house while always knowing that some day I am going to leave. Yes, it will be nice to leave on a schedule." I responded and told him that I was willing to set up a termination date for our work.

The next time when he arrived in my office, he opened the session with the following dream:

> I was at an electric generating plant that had been abandoned. I wanted to go into a building but steps leading to the entrance door were blocked. There were abandoned tools around. My feeling in the dream was that this place represented depression. I thought that this place needed its own energy to be productive. I knew I was going to restore it. I felt good.

After telling me the dream, he reported how joyful he had been the day before. Once more, in the middle of spring, he was noticing green grass, flowers, and warmth. He was full of energy. In his mind, the electric factory was his old self and he alone must re-energize it. "Will I be able to get the electric factory restored and started in a month?" he inquired. I said, "How about three months?" He said, "Okay." The date terminating Hamilton's analysis with me was set.

FOWLER: Hamilton clearly is working at taking stock—he has more memories of a benevolent father. He begins to wonder what he might do after his analysis, and says he would feel comfortable leaving you in a month but wondered if that might be too abrupt of a departure. Now you agree to a termination date. What led you to come to that point?

VOLKAN: For me, a complete analysis requires that the patient goes through stages of growth and has enough experiences with newly developed and/or modified self-representation and the associated ego functions. Throughout the analytic work an analysand deals with resistances, develops and maintains therapeutic alliances, has various therapeutic regressions, works through "hot" transference manifestations and associated mental conflicts, builds new or modified self representation and gains new ego functions, and comes to Oedipal level issues in order to redo them in the transference. During this venture he or she does not follow a straight line.

Imagine the analysand's climbing a flight of stairs. He or she goes up four steps and goes down to the first or second step before climbing up to the fifth step and so on. The analyst also goes down and then up with the analysand. They stay together. The analyst learns to examine his or her emotions and thoughts about changing directions so that he or she does not interfere with such movements and the eventual progress. During these times the analysand "disidentifies" with some of his archaic object images while identifying with the analyst's analyzing function. The analysand, on occasions, still may climb down. But then the analysand and the analyst "sense" that the analysand himself or herself can start thinking about a termination point. At the end the analysand reaches to a place at the top of the stairs. Once he or she looks around to see this new environment, feels secure and comfortable to settle there, and is able to play with everyday life, including its cruelties, without intertwining his or her adult life with the childhood conflicts in obligatory and therefore pathological ways, the analysis comes to an end.

We can make a comparison between a total psychoanalytic process, as described in this book, and Peter Blos' (1979) description of "adolescent passage." Blos called this passage as a "second individuation" process. Early object relations are interwoven with psychic structure formations. Identifications with early objects and their realistic or fantasized functions determine the nature of the child's ego activities and establish the superego forerunners. Following Anna Freud (1958), Blos focuses on modifying of the infantile object ties during adolescence. Similarly during a psychoanalytic process the analysand revisits his early object images, loosens his or her ties to them, and replaces them with idealized ones, or even more aggressively invested ones. At the end he or she finds an "analytic object" in the transference. Identification with this "new object," and its functions become the core identification within the analysand's self-representation. Thus the analysand's previously disturbing object images as well as newly idealized or exaggeratedly aggressive ones become absorbed within this core and lose their power to disturb the analysand's internal world. Revisiting objects of the Oedipal level and modifying them makes the superego more benign. Blos also refers to what happens to "residual trauma" during the adolescent passage. He assumes that trauma "is a universal human condition during infancy and early childhood, leaving, even under the most favorable circumstances, a permanent residue" (p.183). During the adolescent passage the residual trauma "ceases to alert the ego repetitiously via signal anxiety once it has become an integral part of the ego. The residual trauma has become an organizer in the process of character formation" (p.183). During a psychoanalytic process the analysand, like Hamilton, "relives" the childhood traumatic experiences. Thus his or her "residual trauma" shrinks. The analyzed person thus can utilize more adaptive personality traits to deal with the shrunken residual trauma. The youngster who faces an obligatory regression alone during the adolescence goes through a personality modifying experience. This experience sometimes is most useful and sometimes is not useful. An adult analysand who experiences therapeutic regressions and also is "accompanied" by the analyst goes through a better and healthier personally modifying experience, in a sense a more adaptive adolescence passage.

Blos also refers to another developmental challenge during adolescent passage. He believes that a distorted family history, a "family myth," was coercively forced on a child and while going through the adolescent passage the youngster, by direct or indirect ways, re-evaluates his or her family background. This corrective measure restores the integrity of the youngster's senses at least to some degree. During an analytic process, as we had seen in Hamilton's analysis, the "family myth" becomes corrected. Thus a realistic historical continuity for the analysand's identity is provided and the analysand now can use it to know himself or herself better.

Lastly Blos tells us that during the obligatory regression of the adolescent passage there is a chance to have a firmer sexual identity. This also happens during a psychoanalytic process. Certainly Hamilton, who was addicted to "good" women (and was functioning as a "lady's man" for pre-oedipal reasons), became a "mature man" without obligatory urgencies.

What made me agree that Hamilton was ready to finish his analysis? There is no specific rule for this or a specific sign. Obviously the idea that he could finish his analysis did not come to my mind quickly. I have been sensing it and he was sensing it. When he asked to terminate our work together after a month I was ready to say that we could terminate in three months. I was well aware of his original anxieties about separations. I wanted three more months for us to revisit such anxieties if they would come up after the "official" termination date was established. I believe this worked out very well.

Chapter 13
A Blue Ribbon Family

FOWLER: This concludes my conversations with Dr. Volkan. It is fitting to allow Dr. Volkan and Hamilton to complete this story in their way. Questions certainly may arise, but at this stage in the analysis, the hard won gains Hamilton has made will be self-evident. It has been an intriguing and enriching experience to be witness and inquisitor to this process. It is an all too rare opportunity to witness such an intimate and total treatment process.

The day after we set up a date to terminate his analysis, Hamilton came to his session smiling. He said that he was feeling joyful. He liked the idea of my suggesting we work together for three more months. "If you accepted my one month suggestion, I might feel that you did not care. Now we have more room to look around before we stop," he added. Hamilton reported that the night following our setting up the termination date, he dreamed about his father, but in his dream he sensed that the person was really me. He could not recall anything else in the dream. He said that I was in his mind and he would take me to his "electric factory" (of his previous dream), which he would energize. "How do you feel to be kept there?" he asked. I responded by telling him that we had a long and meaningful experience together and in this sense I belong to his "electric factory," and that my image belonged to him as he energizes his "electric factory." I added that I would also keep our experience in my mind. He liked to hear it, but added that he got more from our work together than I did.

Analysands usually deal with two main issues after a date terminating analysis is set. They review their previous personality traits and symptoms as if to say goodbye to them, and they mourn the loss of the analyst. In turn, the analyst changes his or her approach when interpreting the meanings attached to the analysand's free associations, dreams and transference manifestations. Since the analysand worked through such meanings previously, the analyst remains less active as an interpreter and lets the analysand do the job, assume more autonomy, and begin to leave his or her therapeutic regression behind. The analyst, however, also has to mourn letting go of the analysand who, for years, has been an intimate companion.

I sensed that by our setting a date for ending our work together, Hamilton was joyful, but he also perceived a division, as if we drew a line physically separating us. He began to speak about poor Kurds in northern Iraq starving and freezing. But northern Iraq is separated from Turkey by a border. It was clear to me that he was the Kurd and I was the Turk. The emotionally hungry child-Hamilton had returned to my office, and he searched for "nutrition." He did not know if the Turk across the border would help or not. He told me even Dolly had empathy for the poor. A thought occurred to me that "the poor" might also represent me after he stopped paying me and after I lost a "rich" companion. In that case, I would be the Kurd and he would be the Turk. But who would be the Kurd and who would be the Turk, and who would be poor or who would be rich, did not matter. What mattered was that his childhood "emotional" hungry self and corresponding caregiver had returned. Hamilton told me about a woman who had pain in her abdomen. Just before she lost consciousness, she picked up a coloring pen and drew a circle on her skin over the area where she had pain, so the ambulance workers, whom she had called before fainting, would be able to locate the painful area.

I mainly listened to Hamilton without saying much until he told me about the woman who drew a circle on her tummy. Then I asked Hamilton, "Where is your circle?" This was enough for him to "interpret" that his pain was the depressed little Hamilton. He had just brought him symbolically to the office with his reference to the Kurds who were hurt by Saddam Hussein, representing the "bad" parents of his childhood. Then he smiled and reported that he was experiencing very warm feelings toward me. In his mind, I was truly differentiated, he said, from the images of his "whipping parents." Such an experience, he added, was the antidote to prevent the little depressed Hamilton from coming back and dominating his life.

Soon one of his symptoms came for review. When a minor partner in his company was diagnosed with cancer, Hamilton found himself thinking about taking over the man's wife. But such a thought was short-lived and did not lead to any action on his part. When Secretaries Day came, he took several women in his company to a nice restaurant without turning the event into a "pussy pill" collection.

Three weeks after the termination date was set, Hamilton received an invitation from Dorothy to come to Georgia for a family reunion. There were loving sentences in the invitation. Hamilton told me that he felt completely forgiven by his sister. This brought tears to his eyes and then he began sobbing. He kept murmuring, "My father did not believe in crying." Then he added, "But I sometimes cry in the movies." First, I stayed silent so that he could experience his sadness. Then he asked, "Why tears? Why tears?" I answered, "They help us to accept sad realities." He began talking about people who had died and left him. He described his father and mother's graves and then thought of Dolly's death. He gave me more information about his ancestors and informed me that Dolly was 102 years old when she died. At that time, Hamilton was only twenty-nine years old. Ten years before her death, Dolly fell and broke her hip and had surgery, which was not successful. She was bedridden for ten years, but her mind was clear until she died. Describing visits to his bedridden grandmother and her death, Hamilton's voice cracked and he sobbed again. He was saying goodbye to the image of Dolly too.

Hamilton recalled the story of how the Union Forces tore down a church built by his ancestors. After the American Civil War ended in 1865, the family re-built it brick by brick. He reported that he was also building his internal "electric factory" brick by brick. He was very proud of his family background.

Nevertheless, during the next day's session, he visited the "dark side" of the family once more. Then he spoke of how the killing and violence of the Gulf War would live in the minds of the next generations in Iraq, like the events of the American Civil War, he now knew, lived in the minds of generations in the southern United States after 1865. At that time, of course, none of us guessed that Americans—this time during the presidency of Bush's son, George W. Bush—once more would go to war in Iraq about a dozen years later and more war related tragedies would occur.

While Hamilton was reviewing his life for the last time in my office and mourning over his losses and his upcoming loss of me, his business was booming. He had just received a check for two million dollars for a business deal for which his expenses totaled only one million dollars. A few days later, he informed me that some of the money he had just made would go to adding arches to the old house he was renovating and turning into a fancy guest house, in order to give the building a Turkish look. He also planned to use certain wallpapers that would give the interior of the renovated house a Turkish character. Referring to the arches, I told Hamilton that most likely they represented breasts (due to their shape), and that he was internalizing the analyst's breasts, or improving our analytic work through renovating his building (himself). He laughed and informed me that his identification with a "foreign" analyst might also have something to do with his recent dealings with "foreign currencies." He wanted me to know that this investment was a realistic, and indeed, a profitable one. In one of his dreams, he slept with Della. He felt love for her and both were sexy and warm. The next day when he reported his dream, Hamilton cried again. He was mourning once more, this time for his dead wife.

In the middle of the three-month termination phase of Hamilton's analysis, I left Charlottesville for a meeting and Hamilton and I missed three sessions. When we started again, he opened the session with a dream:

> I was in a new house with a handsome front hall. In the hall there was a commode, which was not enclosed. I was urinating. A large stream of urine, yellow, was coming out of me. Yes, I was a little bit embarrassed. But, I was experiencing a great deal of pleasure. Freedom!

Since he was at the termination phase of his analysis, I wanted him to deal with his dreams without my offering any suggestions. After reporting the dream he recalled seeing a French movie about fifteen years ago. In one scene, two men entered a train compartment where a young woman was nursing her baby. She was embarrassed and buttoned up her blouse. One of the men told the woman that his friend was an orphan and that if the woman allowed his friend to suck milk from her breast he would pay her money. At the end, the woman allowed the orphaned man to suck her breast for money.

Soon after reporting his recollection of this scene from the French movie, Hamilton changed the topic and reported that while I was away he had made a lot of money by foreign exchange speculation. When I said nothing, Hamilton "interpreted" what had come to his mind: My leaving him had brought to his mind his old "symptom" concerning his search for a warm breast at the time of a separation from an important other. Instead of feeling anxious or taking some action in search of an idealized woman, he remembered the French movie in which an orphaned adult finds a warm breast. This character represented Hamilton. In the movie, money was needed to obtain the breast for feeding. Hamilton, in reality, had earned a great deal of money recently due to his association with "foreign currency" (the analyst). He said, "I now understand my dream," and then added, "In the past I would search for a breast and also be angry in crazy and murderous ways about losing it. For example, I would squirt my semen on my sister's leg and then expect punishment. This time," he continued, "in my dream huge streams of urine came out of my penis, instead of semen bullets. What a pleasure! What a freedom!" He informed me that his urine was gold color. He recalled how in the past he and I associated "gold" or "money" with feces. Then he repeated, "What a pleasure! What a freedom to urinate or shit without anger and without waiting to be punished." After a while, he reported that in a magazine he had seen another grandfather's advertisement seeking the company of a younger woman. "Poor devil!" he said and laughed again.

During the weekend following this session, he flew to Dorothy's house in Georgia for the family reunion. He had another look at his siblings. Nothing special happened, but things went all right and he felt close to his sister. He reported that in the airplane on the way back to Virginia he said to himself, "Life is good!" Then once more he recalled how his father sent him to a summer camp to learn how to swim. He was then eleven years old and he learned how to swim with the help of a kind instructor. "You also taught me how to swim," he said, and began crying. Then he asked me, "Are there any unresolved things between us?" I told him that if there were such things, they would surface.

Hamilton took a trip to see his younger son and reported to me when he returned that their "bonding" was still very strong. Soon he surprised me by saying that he had talked to Lisa and they mutually agreed to stop seeing each other sexually. According to Hamilton, Lisa had sensed the changes in Hamilton. He was not the same person. Hamilton sometimes sensed that Lisa on occasion perceived him as if he were her alcoholic father and she wanted to change him, such as when she asked him not to drink a glass of wine in restaurants. When Hamilton became well and independent, she began withdrawing from him. On the other hand, Hamilton knew that he would not marry Lisa. Before he finished his analysis he wanted to also finish his relationship with Lisa and be free to find a female partner in the future to whom he could commit himself. Besides, Lisa wanted and was planning to move away from Virginia. And, indeed, she left a week after Hamilton told me about their decision to bring their sexual relationship to an end.

Some ideas came to my mind about why Hamilton chose to separate from Lisa just a couple of weeks before terminating his analysis. Was he repeating the rejection by his mother/Abigail as a review? Was he sending his woman away in order to stay alone with his father/analyst and identify with him further? I also wondered if I should bring such thoughts out in the open so late in his analysis. First, I said nothing. The day Lisa left Virginia, Hamilton, on the couch, reported his feeling of being abandoned. I almost told him that he might be repeating a rejection scene for a last review, when Hamilton spoke and told me that he had been analyzing his reasons for breaking up in a friendly and mutual way with Lisa. "I wanted to know if it would be easy and indeed nice to give up a woman," he added. There was, therefore, nothing for me to say.

Next, he told me he had been looking at some pictures of a volcanic scene (Volkan) on the island of Maui and he perceived that this place was desolate-looking, representing loneliness. He wondered if I would miss him. I responded, "Yes." He smiled and said, "I know you will be able to survive without me . . . " and then completed his sentence: "I will be able to survive without you."

During one session just before his analysis came to an end, he told me that the day before, his older son's wife had taken her children to a country fair and they had come home with "Blue Ribbons" they won for competitions they had entered. Hamilton visited them that night and observed, with pride and joy, his happy grandchildren. He said to me, "During my analysis I told you the stories of six generations of my family, from the generation that lived through the American Civil War to the generation of my grandchildren. The psychic health of the Hamilton family has improved. I see myself as a bridge on which a proud but traumatized Virginia family passed to a brighter future. Thank you for your help to build this bridge." I was moved.

Hamilton put his hand into his jacket pocket and pulled out two photographs and while still lying on the couch gave me the photographs and wanted me to look at them. In them Hamilton, with a big smile on his face, was surrounded by happy children, his grandchildren. I gave the pictures back to him and thanked him for introducing me to his grandchildren. With pride in his voice and tears in his eyes, Hamilton said, "I have 'Blue Ribbon' grandchildren."

He was so emotional that he could not continue to speak. Both of us stayed silent until he collected himself and began to talk about how one of his favorite restaurants where he frequently ate lunch had changed hands and from now on it would be closed for lunch. This was all right with him, he added, since he would enjoy trying new places. Suddenly he realized that he was talking about us. My couch would be "closed" for him and he would try new places. I could see that he felt sad and I, too, felt sad.

When Hamilton arrived for his last session, four years and ten months after we first met, he asked me a question as soon as he closed my office door behind him: "Do I lay on the couch during my last hour?" I said that it would be fine with me if he chose to sit on a chair. He chose to take his usual position on the couch, saying, "I'll be on my feet when I leave you!"

He spoke of my using the phrase "It is written." During the early part of his analysis, when his internal world made him repeat certain patterns in his daily life, I used this phrase more than once to explain to him how his neurosis was like his own personal Holy Book in that his repertoire of rituals were written and that he felt obliged to follow them. Hamilton explained how much he appreciated my "it is written" phrase because it had helped him to understand the power of his psychopathology and later work on it and leave it behind. He then gave me some examples of his changes. One of his junior partners who had cancer was not doing well, and Hamilton was concerned about him without having any sexual interest in his wife. He added, "Perhaps a perfect woman belongs to someone else." He then recalled seeing me at a theater with an obese woman. He told me that maybe I should change "my woman" and find a "perfect woman." I knew that he was visiting the "it is written" phenomenon and the influence of his previous neurosis. He would keep alive a little bit of his neurosis by giving it to me. I said to him, "It is written! Take it back! If you give whatever is left of your neurosis to me, it will still be alive. Do you want me to stomp on a cabbage?" Hamilton laughed and laughed. "I knew what I was doing," he said. "I recognized it."

He ended up saying, "It is not necessary to find a perfect woman, and it is not necessary to be perfect." He kept laughing like a child who had figured out that something that had startled him was not really dangerous.

Hamilton said to me, "I now want to tell you about the recent 'American dollar' and 'Foreign currency' interactions." I stopped him by saying, " . . . which leads to . . . " He responded "to us!" Then he added, "Once I was hoping for a perfect analysis. Now I know that you are not perfect and I am not perfect." This time I smiled and responded to him, "What a relief!" He spontaneously repeated after me, " What a relief!" We both stayed silent. We had another ten more minutes to end his last session. I think both of us knew that there was nothing more to say. He got up from my couch before our time ran out and I got up from my chair. He shook my hand firmly and left.

Chapter 14
Years Later

For five years after Hamilton finished his analysis, I had no contact with him. This did not surprise me at all. Typically, after a successful analysis, analysands do not call their analysts. I knew that he was still living in Richmond because now and then I came across his name in a Richmond newspaper, which was also distributed in Charlottesville. During this time, I slowly withdrew from practicing psychoanalysis and began devoting more and more time to understanding the psychology of international affairs, large-group (i.e., ethnic groups) aggression, political leader-follower interactions and in developing interdisciplinary and psychoanalytically informed methods for "unofficial diplomacy" (Volkan, 1988, 1997, 2004a, 2006a). Thus, I traveled a lot to various parts of the world and spent a great deal of time away from Charlottesville.

One day, five years after Hamilton and I finished working together, I attended the wedding in Charlottesville of the daughter of family friends. After the wedding ceremony, we went to a country club for the reception. Suddenly at the other end of the huge crowded room where this event was taking place, I saw Hamilton. His physical appearance had not changed much. When he saw me he excitedly grabbed the hand of a nice-looking woman, perhaps in her fifties, and pulled her behind him. Both of them, almost running, and pushing their way through the crowd, came to me. He shook my hand and then, turning to the woman accompanying him and at the same time pointing at me, he said to her, "My analyst! My analyst!" He did not even refer to my name; I was simply his analyst. The woman then, with a big smile, shook my hand, told me her name and added, "I am Hamilton's wife. I am so pleased to meet you. Hamilton told me how grateful he is to you. Thank you. Thank you. We are very, very happy." Then she and her husband left and disappeared into the crowd. I realized that with the excitement of the moment I had not caught Mrs. Hamilton's first name. I did not know if she was one of his previous girlfriends or someone whom he met after he finished his analysis. A thought occurred to me that whoever she was, she was not a "perfect woman" since she said they were very, very happy and since both of them appeared to me to be so happy.

After this event, I never saw Hamilton again, but continued to see his name here and there for over a dozen years after we stopped working together, and a couple of years ago I learned that he had retired and moved with his wife to a resort area. My last glimpse of him, after he introduced me to his wife, was in the crowded room of the wedding party. He and his wife were holding hands as if they were young lovers.

Bibliography

Abend, S. "Countertransference, Empathy, and the Analytic Ideal: The Impact of Life Stresses on Analytic Capability." *Psychoanalytic Quarterly,* 55 (1986): 563-575.

Abse, P.W. and J.A. Ewing. "Some Problems in Psychotherapy with Schizophrenic Patients." *American Journal of Psychotherapy,* 14 (1960): 505-519.

Alexander, F. and T. M. French. *Psychoanalytic Therapy: Principles and Application.* New York: The Ronald Press, 1946.

Alptekin, G. "Rüya ve aktarım: Analistin görüldügü ilk rüya." *Dream and Transference: The First Dream in Which Analyst Appears.* In *Psikoanalitik Bakışlar: Akltarım-Karsıaktarım (Psychoanalytic Views: Transference-Countertransference),* Pp. 153-165. Istanbul: PPPD Yayınları (2006).

Andrews, S. C. and J. P. Fenton. "Archeology and the Invisible Man: The Role of Slavery in the Production of Wealth and Social Class in the Bluegrass Region of Kentucky, 1820 to 1870." *World Archeology,* 33 (2001): 115.

Arlow, J. "Unconscious Fantasy and Disturbances of Conscious Experience." *Psychoanalytic Quarterly,* 38 (1969): 1-27.

———. "Motivations for Peace." Pp. 193-204 in *Psychological Basis of War,* edited by H.Z. Winnik, R. Moses, and M. Ostow. Jerusalem: Jerusalem Academic Press, 1973.

Beres, D. "The Unconscious Fantasy." *Psychoanalytic Quarterly,* 31 (1962): 309-329.

Bergmann, M.V. "Thoughts on Super-Ego Pathology of Survivors and Their Children." Pp. 287-311 in *Generations of the Holocaust,* edited by M.S. Bergmann and M.E. Jucovy. New York: Basic Books 1982.

Blos, P. *The Adolescent Passage: Developmental Issues.* New York: International Universities Press, 1979.

Blum, H. P. "Acting Out, the Psychoanalytic Process, and Interpretation." *Annals of Psychoanalysis,* 4 (1976): 163-184.

———. "Superego Formation, Adolescent Transformation and the Adult Neurosis." *Journal of the American Psychoanalytic Association,* 4 (1985): 887-909.

Boesky, D. "Acting Out: A Reconsideration of the Concept." *International Journal of Psycho-Analysis,* 63 (1982): 39-59.

Boyer, L.B. *The Regressed Patient.* New York: Jason Aronson, 1983.

Brenner, I. "Returning to the Fire: Surviving the Holocaust and 'Going Back.'" *Journal of Applied Psychoanalytic Studies,* 1 (1999): 145-162.

Cain, A. C. and B.S. Cain. "On Replacing a Child." *Journal of the American Academy of Child Psychiatry,* 3 (1964): 443-456.

Eckstaedt, I. *Nationalismus in der "zweiten Generation:" Psychoanalyse von Hörigkeitsverhältnissen (National Socialism in the Second Generation: Psychoanalysis of Master-SlaveRelationships).* Frankfurt: A. M.: Suhrkamp Verlag (1989).

Erikson, E.H. *Identity and Life Cycle.* New York: International University Press, 1950.

———. *Insight and Responsibility.* New York: W. W. Norton, 1964.

———. *Childhood and Society.* New York: W. W. Norton, 1985.

Fogel, R. W. and S. L. Engerman. *Time on the Cross: The Economics of American Negro Slavery.* New York: W. W. Norton & Company, 1995.

Follet, R. "Heat, Sex, and Sugar; Pregnancy and Childbearing in the Slave Quarters." *Journal of Family History,* 28 (2003): 510-539.

Frankl, V. E. *Man's Search for Meaning: An Introduction to Logotherapy.* Oxford, England: Washington Square Press, 1963.

Freud, A. "The Widening Scope of Indications for Psychoanalysis: Discussion." *Journal of the American Psychoanalytic Association,* 2 (1954): 607-620.

———. "Adolescence." *The Psychoanalytic Study of the Child,* 13 (1958): 255-278.

Freud, A. and D. Burlingham. *War and Children.* Oxford, England, 1943.

Freud, S. (1908). "On Hysterical Phantasies and Their Relation to Bisexuality." *Standard Edition,* 9: 155-166. London: Hogarth Press, 1959.

———. (1912). "The Dynamics of Transference." *Standard Edition,* 12: 99-108. London: Hogarth Press, 1959.

———. (1914). "Remembering, Repeating and Working Through." *Standard Edition,* 12: 147—156. London: Hogarth Press, 1958.

———. (1925). "Psycho-Analytic Notes on an Autobiographical Account of a Case of Paranoia (Dementia Paranoids)." *Standard Edition,* 12: 3-82; London: Hogarth Press, 1958.

———. (1932) "Why War?" *Standard Edition,* 22:197-215; London: Hogarth Press, 1964.

Fromm, G. M. "A View from Riggs: Treatment Resistance and Patient Authority-II. Transmission of Trauma and Treatment Resistance." *Journal of the American Academy of Psychoanalysis and Dynamic Psychiatry,* 34 (2006): 445-458.

Giovacchini, P. *Treatment of Primitive Mental States.* New York: Jason Aronson, 1979.

Grubrich-Simitis, I. "Extremtraumatisierung als kumulatives Trauma: Psychoanalytische Studien über seelische Nachwirkungen der Konzentrationslagerhaft bei Überlebenden und ihren Kindern." (Extreme traumatization as a cumulative trauma: Psychoanalytic studies on the mental effects of imprisionment in concentration camps on survivors and their children). *Psyche* 33 (1979): 991-1023.

Gutman, H. G. *Slavery and the Numbers Game: A Critique of Time on the Cross*. Chicago: University of Illinois Press, 2003.

Inderbitzin, L.B. and S.T. Levy. "Unconscious Fantasy: A Reconsideration of the Concept." *Journal of the American Psychoanalytic Association*, 38 (1990): 113-130.

Israëls, H. (1989*)*. *Schreber: Father and Son*. Trans. from Dutch, H. S. Lake. Amsterdam: Elandsstraat, 1981, 127.

Jacobson, E. "Transference Problems in the Psychoanalytic Treatment of Severely Depressive Patients." *Journal of the American Psychoanalytic Association*, 2 (1954): 595-606.

———. *The Self and the Object World.* New York: International Universities Press, 1964.

Jokl, A.M. *Zwei Fällezum Thema Bewaltigung der Vergangeheit (Two cases referring to the theme of "mastering the past")*. Frankfurt A.M.: Jüdischer Verlag (1997).

Kernberg, O.F. *Object Relations Theory and Clinical Psychoanalysis.* New York: Jason Aronson, 1976.

———. *Internal World and External Reality.* New York: Jason Aronson, 1980.

Kestenberg, J. S. and I. Brenner. *The Last Witness: The Child Survivor of the Holocaust.* Washington, DC: American Psychiatric Press, 1996.

Kogan, I. *Der Stumme Schrei der Kinder-Die zweite Generation der Holocaust Opfer* (*The Cry of Mute Children — The Second Generation of the Holocaust*). Frankfurt: S. Fischer, 1998.

———. "Breaking the Cycle of Trauma: From the Individual to Society." *Mind and Human Interaction,* 11 (2000): 2-10.

———. "The Role of the Analyst in the Analytic Cure During Times of Chronic Crises." *Journal of the American Psychoanalytic Association,* 52 (2004): 735-757.

Kubie, L.S. *Practical and Theoretical Aspects of Psychoanalysis.* New York: International Universities Press, 1950.

Leowald, H. "On the Therapeutic Action of Psychoanalysis." *Journal of the Psychoanalytic Association,* 41 (1960): 16-33.

Mahler, M.S. *On Human Symbiosis and the Vicissitudes of Individuation.* New York: International Universities Press, 1968.

Modell, A.H. "A Narcissistic Defense Against Affects and the Illusion of Self-Sufficiency." *International Journal of Psychoanalysis,* 56 (1975): 275-282.

Novey, S. *The Second Look: The Reconstruction of Personal History in Psychiatry and Psychoanalysis*. Baltimore: John Hopkins Press, 1968.

Olinick, S.L. *The Therapeutic Instrument.* New York: Jason Aronson, 1980.

Poznanski, E. O. "The Replacement Child": A Saga of Unrecorded Parental Grief. *Behavioral Pediatrics,* 81 (1972): 1190-1193.

Pyles, R. L. "The Good Fight: Psychoanalysis During the Age of Managed Care." *Journal of the American Psychoanalytic Association,* 51 (Supplement) (2003): 23-41.

Rapaport, E. "The First Dream in an Erotized Transference." *International Journal of Psycho-Analysis* 40 (1959): 240-245.

Renik, O. "Playing One's Cards Face Up in Analysis: An Approach to the Problem of Self-Disclosure." *Psychoanalytic Quarterly, 68* (1999): 521-530.

Saul, L. J and E. Sheppard. "An Attempt to Quantify Emotional Forces Using Manifest Dreams: a Preliminary Study." *Journal of American Psychoanalytic Association* (1956): 486-502.

Schreber, D. G. M. *Das Buch den Gesundheit: Eine Orthobiotik nach den Gesetzen der Natur und Baue des menschlichen Organismus.* (*The Book of Health*). Leipzig: Oswald Mutze (1893).

———. (1903) *Denkwürdigkeiten eines Nervenkranken nebst Nachtragen und einem Anhang über die Frage:Unter welchen Voraussetzungen darf eine für geisteskrank erachtete Person gegen ihren erklärten Willen in einer Heilanstalt festgehalten werden? (Memories of My Nervous Illness*). Leipzig: Oswald Mutze.

Stone, L. "The Widening Scope for Psychoanalysis." *Journal of the American Psychoanalytic Association,* 2 (1954): 567-594.

Streeck-Fischer, A. "Naziskins in Germany: How Traumatization Deals with the Past." *Mind and Human Interaction,* 110 (1999): 84-97.

Tähkä, V. "Dealing with Object Loss." *Scandinavian Psychoanalytic Review,* 7 (1984): 13-33.

Varvin, S. and Volkan, V. D. eds. *Violence or Dialogue: Psychoanalytic Insights on Terror and Terrorism.* London: International Psychoanalytical Association, 2003.

Volkan, V.D. *Primitive Internalized Object Relations: A Clinical Study of Schizophrenic, Borderline and Narcissistic Patients.* New York: International Universities Press, 1976.

———. "The 'Glass Bubble' of the Narcissistic Patient." Pp. 405-431, in *Advances in Psychotherapy of the Borderline Patient,* edited by Joseph LeBoit and Attilio Capponi. New York: Jason Aronson, 1979.

———. "Transference and Countertransference: An Examination from the Point of View of Internalized Object Relations." Pp. 429-451 in *Object and Self: A Developmental Approach (Essays in Honor of Edith Jacobson),* edited. by S. Tuttman, C. Kaye and M. Zimmerman. New York: International Universities Press, 1981.

———. *What Do You Get When You Cross a Dandelion With a Rose?: The True Story of a Psychoanalysis.* New York: Jason Aronson, 1984.

———. *Six Steps in the Treatment of Borderline Personality Organization.* Northvale, NJ: Jason Aronson, 1987.

———. *The Need to Have Enemies and Allies: From Clinical Practice to International Relationships*. Northvale, NJ: Jason Aronson, 1988.

———. *The Infantile Psychotic Self: Understanding and Treating Schizophrenics and Other Difficult Patients*. Northvale, NJ: Jason Aronson, 1995.

———. *Bloodlines: From Ethnic Pride to Ethnic Terrorism*. New York: Farrar, Straus and Giroux, 1997.

———. *Blind Trust: Large Groups and Their Leaders in Times of Crises and Terror*. Charlottesville, VA: Pitchstone Publishing, 2004a.

———. "Actualized Unconscious Fantasies and 'Therapeutic Play in Adults' Analyses: Further Study of These Concepts." In *Power of Understanding: Essays in Honour of Veikko Tähkä*, ed. A. Laine, 119-141. London: Karnac Books, 2004b.

———. *Killing in the Name of Identity: Stories of Bloody Conflicts*. Charlottesville, VA: Pitchstone Publishing, 2006a.

———. "Psikodinâmica da violência de grandes grupas e da violência de massas." *Ciência & Saúde Coletiva*, (Large-group psychodynamics and massive violence) 11 (2006b): 303-314.

Volkan, V.D. and Ast, G. *Spektrum des Narzißmus: Eine klinische Studie des gesunden Narzißmus, des narzißtisch-masochistischen Charakters, der narzißtischen Persönlichkeitsorganisation, des malignen Narzißmus und des erfolgreichen Narzißmus*. (*Spectrum of Narcissism: A Clinical Study of Healthy Narcissism, Narcissistic-Masochistic Character, Narcissistic Personality-Organization, Malignant Narcissism, and Successful Narcissism*.) Göttingen: Vandenhoeck & Ruprecht, (1994).

Volkan, V. D. and G. Ast. *Siblings in the Unconscious and Psychopathology*. Madison, CT: International Universities Press, 1997.

Volkan, V. D., G. Ast. and W. F Greer. *The Third Reich in the Unconscious: Transgenerational Transmission and its Consequences*. New York: Brunner-Routledge, 2002.

Volkan, V. D. & N. Itzkowitz. *The Immortal Atatürk: A Psychobiography*. Chicago: University of Chicago Press, 1984.

Weigert, E. "The Importance of Flexibility in Psychoanalytic Technique." *Journal of the American Psychoanalytic Association*, 2 (1954): 702-710.

Werner, H. and B. Kaplan. *Symbol Formation*. New York: Wiley, 1963.

Index

About the Authors

Vamık D. Volkan, M.D. is the Senior Erik Erikson Scholar at the Erikson Institute of Education and Research of the Austen Riggs Center, Stockbridge, Massachusetts, an Emeritus Professor of Psychiatry at the University of Virginia, Charlottesville, VA, an Emeritus Training and Supervising Analyst at the Washington Psychoanalytic Institute, Washington, D.C. and a guest lecturer at the Berkshire Psychoanalytic Institute, Stockbridge, MA. He is a recipient of the Sigmund Freud Award given by the city of Vienna in collaboration with the World Council of Psychotherapy, was a "Fulbright/Sigmund-Freud-Privatstiftung Visiting Scholar of Psychoanalysis" in Vienna, Austria and a Visiting Professor at the Institute of Political Science, the University of Vienna. He holds Honorary Doctorate degrees from Kuopio University, Finland and from the Ankara University, Turkey. He is the author or co-author of over 30 books and the editor or co-editor of 10 more. His work has been translated into many languages. He was a founder and a president of both the International Society of Political Psychology (ISPP) and the Virginia Psychoanalytic Society and the president of the American College of Psychoanalysts.

J. Christopher Fowler, Ph.D. is the Director of Research at the Erik H. Erikson Institute of the Austen Riggs Center. He is a Fellow of the Society for Personality Assessment, Consulting Editor for the *Journal of Personality Assessment*, and a member of the Society for Psychotherapy Research. Dr. Fowler has written and co-authored over forty articles and book chapters on personality assessment, suicide risk, long-term psychoanalytically-oriented residential treatment for severely disturbed patients, psychotherapy outcome studies, and psychodynamic interviewing.

www.ingramcontent.com/pod-product-compliance
Ingram Content Group UK Ltd.
Pitfield, Milton Keynes, MK11 3LW, UK
UKHW012041150926
475560UK00001B/123

9 780765 706164